LOGIC

Logic: The Basics is a hands-on introduction to the philosophically alive field of logical inquiry. Covering both classical and non-classical theories, it presents some of the core notions of logic such as validity, basic connectives, identity, 'free logic' and more. This book:

- introduces some basic ideas of logic from a semantic and philosophical perspective
- uses logical consequence as the focal concept throughout
- considers some of the controversies and rival logics that make for such a lively field.

This accessible guide includes chapter summaries and suggestions for further reading as well as exercises and sample answers throughout. It is an ideal introduction for those new to the study of logic as well as those seeking to gain the competence and skills needed to move to more advanced work in logic.

Jc Beall is Professor of Philosophy at the University of Connecticut, USA, where he is Director of the UConn Logic Group. His books include *Possibilities and Paradox: An Introduction to Modal and Many-Valued Logic* with Bas van Fraassen, *Logical Pluralism* with Greg Restall, and *Spandrels of Truth*.

THE BASICS

LOGIC

THE BASICS

jc beall

Routledge
Taylor & Francis Group

LONDON AND NEW YORK

First published 2010
by Routledge
2 Park Square, Milton Park, Abingdon, Oxon. OX14 4RN

Simultaneously published in the USA and Canada by
Routledge
270 Madison Avenue, New York, NY 10016

Routledge is an imprint of the Taylor & Francis Group, an informa business

© 2010 Jc Beall

Typeset in LATEX by the author
Printed and bound in Great Britain by TJ International Ltd, Padstow, Cornwall

British Library Cataloguing in Publication Data
A catalogue record for this book is available from the British Library

Library of Congress Cataloging in Publication Data
Beall, J. C.
   Logic : the basics / J.C. Beall.
      p. cm. – (The basics)
   Includes bibliographical references and index.
   1. Logic. I. Title.
   BC108.B347 2010
   160–dc22

                    2009046227

ISBN 10: 0-415-77498-5 (hbk)
ISBN 10: 0-415-77499-3 (pbk)
ISBN 10: 0-203-85155-2 (ebk)

ISBN 13: 978-0-415-77498-7 (hbk)
ISBN 13: 978-0-415-77499-4 (pbk)
ISBN 13: 978-0-203-85155-5 (ebk)

For Katrina Higgins – for everything.
And for Charles & Beverly Beall – for everything else.

PREFACE

A book should have either intelligibility or correctness;
to combine the two is impossible.
– Bertrand Russell (1901)

This book presents a few basic ideas in logical studies, particularly some ideas in philosophical logic—logic motivated largely by philosophical issues. The book aims not only to introduce you to various ideas and logical theories; it aims to give you a flavor for logical theorizing—theorizing about logic in the face of apparently logic-relevant phenomena. If the book is successful, you'll not only be in position to pursue logic at a deeper level; you'll be motivated to do so.

The book takes a wholly one-sided approach to logic: namely, the so-called 'semantic' or 'model-theoretic' side. You should be warned: there is much, much more to logic than is found—or even hinted at—in this book. A particularly conspicuous omission is so-called proof theory: no 'deductive systems' of any sort are discussed in this book. This omission is unfortunate in various ways but—given space limitations on this book—it allows a more leisurely discussion of a wider array of ideas than would otherwise be possible. A handful of widely available 'further readings' are suggested throughout, and a few them—namely, ones that are repeatedly mentioned—provide adequate proof systems for the canvassed logics (model-theoretically understood).

Unsolicited advice to readers

This book is intended to be read in order, with each chapter presupposing its predecessors. If you've already had some elementary logic training, some of the early chapters can be skipped; however, the book is intended chiefly for those who have had very little, if any, logic training.

While mastering them often requires patience and careful thinking, logical ideas are often fairly intuitive. Usually, when an idea initially seems hard or too abstract, a bit more thinking will eventually do the trick. My advice is that in times of initial difficulty you give the matter a bit more thought. Moreover, don't just work to master the given matters. Try hard to think about *different logical options* from those explicitly canvassed in the book. For example (though this won't make much sense before you read a few chapters), if a theory claims that the 'right logic' works *this* way, try to think about an alternative theory according to which the 'right logic' works *that* way. The benefit of such alternative thinking is two-fold: you'll get the chance to do some logical theorizing on your own, and perhaps even come up with a new logical theory; and, more importantly, the exploration will probably be quite enjoyable, no matter how hard you have to think.

Unsolicited advice to teachers

This book has been used successfully in three different classroom settings.

- *First course in logic.* The text has been used as a fairly gentle introduction to logical studies for all manner of majors (science and humanities/arts), supplemented with handouts giving adequate 'proof systems' (e.g., tableau or natural deduction). Many students often go on to do a regular classical first-order logic course, and then proceed to do further studies, either as a major or minor, in philosophy or philosophical logic.

- *Supplement to philosophy of logic.* The text has been used as a required supplemental text in introductory and advanced philosophy of logic courses. In such courses, the focus is the *philosophy* of logic(s), with this book providing some of the *logical* ideas that feed the philosophy.

- *Early (post-) graduate course.* The text has been used as a sort of transition text for students entering analytic programs in philosophy. In this capacity, the text is used as a source of basic logical ideas, with a slant on philosophically motivated logical ideas, and is usually used as a predecessor to much more in-depth study of philosophical logic (i.e., formal logics motivated by philosophy).

Despite such success, the book can undoubtedly be improved, and teachers are hereby encouraged to send suggestions for improvement. (Note that a supplemental manual of answers—and other material—may be made available to teachers.)

Brief history of the book

I was invited to write a book on logic for the Routledge *Basics* series, which I think is a good and useful series, and I was happy to contribute. The trouble—as logicians and logic teachers will know—is that the universe cannot possibly fit another introductory logic textbook; it is already overly stuffed, indeed bursting to rid itself of elementary logic texts. As a result, this book was *not* to be—and, given the state of the universe, could not be—another introductory logic textbook. And so it isn't. On the other hand, the book was not to be another 'logic for dummies' or picture-book presentation of logical ideas. (Actually, the latter would've been good, but, alas, I didn't—and still don't—know how to do it.) Instead, the book was to give at least a bit of 'real logical content' for those wanting to introduce themselves to aspects of logical theorizing; and the book was to do so with the goal of breadth over depth; but, again, there was to be 'real content', and so breadth had to suffer a little bit while depth had to be deep enough—but not too deep.

What you have before you is my first attempt to do what was to be done. Though it was not my aim when I set about writing the chapters, I found it difficult not to conform to earlier ideas expressed in some of my previous work. This is particularly the case with *Logical Pluralism* (2005), which I wrote with my friend and longstanding logical colleague Greg Restall. That book—namely, *Logical Pluralism*—is suggested as further reading for those who wish to pursue the *philosophy* of logic, and in particular the philosophy of logical rivalry, in more depth. While philosophical issues motivate *this* book's contents, the philosophy of logic is barely discussed.

The tension between breadth, depth, and short-but-intelligible is a challenging constraint. My hope, in the end, is as above: that this book not only prepares you for deeper, more detailed logical study, but that it motivates you to do so.

Miscellany

'Further reading' sections, found at the end of each chapter, attempt *not* to be historical remarks, but rather only pointers to either very broad survey-like material, wherein fuller bibliographic references are found, or more advanced work that is nonetheless fairly accessible and full of adequate bibliographical pointers.

I refer to whole chapters using 'Chapter n', where n is the given chapter number. I refer to proper parts of chapters (viz., sections or subsections) using '§$n.m$', which may be read 'section m of Chapter n'.

Throughout this book, unless otherwise noted, the word 'or' is used in its so-called inclusive usage, which amounts to *either... or... or both*. Reminders are sometimes given about this, but it's useful to take note now (so as to avoid confusion with the so-called exclusive usage, which involves the *not-both* reading).

Also, mostly for space-saving reasons (or avoiding an otherwise bad line break), the abbreviation 'st' for *such that* is sometimes used, though mostly in late chapters. (It is also usually flagged and explained again when used.) Similarly, the standard 'iff' abbreviation for *if and only if* is frequently used, and is explained in Chapter 1.

« *Parenthetical remark.* I should note one other bit of style. In a few places, so-called parenthetical remarks are displayed in the way that this parenthetical remark is displayed. This convention is used in a few places where either footnotes would otherwise be too long or there are already too many footnotes in the given area. *End parenthetical.* »

ACKNOWLEDGEMENTS

Always be thankful. And mean it.
– Dee Dee Long

I am grateful to many people for discussions and lessons that are reflected in this book. Some of those people are as follows (I would say 'all' were it not for inadvertent omissions): Jeff Blocker, Ross Brady, Phillip Bricker, Otávio Bueno, Colin Caret, Colin Cheyne, Matt Clemens, Mark Colyvan, Roy Cook, Aaron Cotnoir, Max Cresswell, Charlie Donahue, Hartry Field, Jay Garfield, Chris Gauker, Ed Gettier, Rod Girle, Michael Glanzberg, Geoff Goddu, Patrick Greenough, Patrick Grim, Gary Hardegree, Ole Hjortland, Michael Hughes, Dominic Hyde, Carrie Jenkins, the late David Lewis, Michael Lynch, Maureen Malley, Ed Mares, the late Maximum Leader (viz., Bob Meyer), Chris Mortensen, Daniel Nolan, Doug Owings, Graham Priest, Agustín Rayo, Stephen Read, Greg Restall, David Ripley, Marcus Rossberg, Gill Russell, Josh Schechter, Jerry Seligman, Lionel Shapiro, Stewart Shapiro, John Slaney, Nick (J. J.) Smith, Reed Solomon, David Steuber, Koji Tanaka, Richard Trammell, Bas van Fraassen, Achillé Varzi, David Villa, Vũ, Zach Weber, Sam Wheeler, Robbie Williams, Jeremy Wyatt, Nicole Wyatt, Crispin Wright, and Paul Zumbo.

I am very grateful to some people who gave helpful feedback on earlier drafts: Aaron Cotnoir, Chris Gauker, Greg Restall, David Steuber, Jeremy Wyatt, Paul Zumbo, and five additional anonymous readers for Routledge. Michael Hughes provided useful comments on both an early and a late draft, and I'm grateful for his help. Also, Dave Ripley gave particularly good and useful comments on a late draft; I am very grateful for Dave's insights, and equally grateful for his enthusiasm with respect to this project. For a variety of reasons (most schedule-related), some rather good suggestions from these readers have been left out. I hope, nevertheless, that the book remains useful and interesting.

Marcus Rossberg provided not only useful discussion of logical and philosophical issues; he also provided some help in thinking about and working out some LaTeX issues in conforming to some Routledge style demands.

I am grateful to David Villa and Maureen Malley, who each caught a few errors at the last moment. Villa and Malley and their 2211Q classmates were generally helpful—and I hereby express gratitude.

With respect to LaTeX I join many authors in being greatly indebted to the genius and generosity of the LaTeX pioneers and subsequent LaTeX community. Thank you, all of you.

Finally, this book is dedicated to Katrina Higgins and Charles & Beverly Beall. The three of them, jointly and in their own individual ways, are responsible for my seeking alternative logical lands. And that has made all the difference.

Jc Beall
Storrs, 2009

CONTENTS

PART I

BACKGROUND IDEAS

1

Consequences

> *Everybody, sooner or later,*
> *sits down to a banquet of consequences.*
> – Robert Louis Stevenson

'Watch what you say,' my mother often advised, 'because what you say has consequences.' She was right, and doubly so. There are two senses in which what one says has consequences. One sense, not terribly relevant for present purposes, is captured in the familiar dictum that actions have consequences. To say something is to do something, and doing something is an action. Actions, in turn, are events, and events, as experience tells, have consequences, namely, their causal effects. (Example: a consequence— a causal effect—of your drinking petrol is your being ill, at least other things being equal.) So, in the *causal effects* sense of 'consequences', my mother was perfectly right, but that sense of 'consequence' has little to do with logic.

For present purposes, there is a more relevant sense in which what one says has consequences. What one says, at least in the declarative mode,[1] has *logical consequences*, namely, whatever *logically follows from* what one said, or whatever is *logically implied* by what one said. Suppose, for example, that you're given the following information.

1. Agnes is a cat.

2. All cats are smart.

---

[1] For purposes of this book, a *declarative sentence* (or a sentence used in the 'declarative mode') is one that is used (successfully or otherwise) to declare or state something about the world. This is hardly a precise definition, but it'll do. (Example. Each of 'You are reading a book', 'Obama is the first black US president', and '1+1=5' are declarative sentences, but sentences such as 'Shut that door!' and 'Do you like Vegemite?' are not declarative, since they fail to declare or state anything about the world.)

A consequence of (1) and (2), taken together, is that Agnes is smart. In other words, *that Agnes is smart* logically follows from (1) and (2); it is implied by (1) and (2), taken together.

1.1 Relations of support

Logical consequence is a relation on sentences of a language, where 'sentence', unless otherwise indicated, is short for 'meaningful, declarative sentence'.[2]

Logical consequence is one among many relations over the sentences of a language. Some of those relations might be called *relations of support.* For example, let $A_1, \ldots, A_n$ and B be arbitrary sentences of some given language—say, English. For some such sentences, the various A_i jointly 'support' B in the following sense.

S1. If all of $A_1, \ldots, A_n$ are true, then B is *probably* true.

Consider, for example, the following sentences.

3. Max took a nap on Day 1.
4. Max took a nap on Day 2.
5. Max took a nap on Day 3.

   $\vdots$

n. Max took a nap on Day n (viz., today).

m. Max will take a nap on Day $n + 1$ (viz., tomorrow).

On the surface, sentences (3)–(n) support sentence (m) in the sense of (S1): the former, taken together, make the latter more likely. Similarly, (6) supports (7) in the same way.

6. The sun came up every day in the past.
7. The sun will come up tomorrow.

If (6) is true, then (7) is probably true too.

The relation of support given in (S1) is important for empirical science and, in general, for rationally navigating about our world. Clarifying the (S1) notion of 'support' is the job of probability theory (and, relatedly, decision theory), an area beyond the range of this book.

---

[2]Taking consequence to be relation on sentences simplifies matters a great deal, and sidesteps the issue of so-called 'truth bearers', an ongoing issue in philosophy of logic. For present purposes, simplicity is worth the sidestep.

1.2   Logical consequence: the basic recipe

Logical consequence, the chief topic of logic, is a stricter relation of support than that in (S1). Notice, for example, that while (7) may be very likely true if (6) is true, it is still possible, in some sense, for (6) to be true without (7) being true. After all, the sun might well explode later today.

While (S1) might indicate a strong relation of support between some sentences and another, it doesn't capture the tightest relation of support. Logical consequence, on many standard views, is often thought to be the tightest relation of support over sentences of a language. In order for some sentence B to be a logical consequence of sentences $A_1, \ldots, A_n$, the truth of the latter needs to 'guarantee' the truth of the former, in some suitably strong sense of 'guarantee'.

Throughout this book, we will rely on the following (so-called semantic) account of logical consequence, where $A_1, \ldots, A_n$ and B are arbitrary sentences of some given language (or fragment of a language).

Definition 1. (Logical Consequence) *B is a logical consequence of $A_1, \ldots, A_n$ if and only if there is no case in which $A_1, \ldots, A_n$ are all true but B is not true.*

Notice that the given 'definition' has two parts corresponding to the 'if and only if' construction, namely,

- If B is a logical consequence of $A_1, \ldots, A_n$, then there is no case in which $A_1, \ldots, A_n$ are all true but B is not true.
- If there is no case in which $A_1, \ldots, A_n$ are all true but B is not true, then B is a logical consequence of $A_1, \ldots, A_n$.

Also notable is that the given 'definition' is really just a recipe. In order to get a proper definition, one needs to specify two key ingredients:

- what 'cases' are;
- what it is to be *true in a case.*

Once these ingredients are specified, one gets an account of logical consequence. For example, let $A_1, \ldots, A_n$ and B be declarative sentences of English. If we have a sufficiently precise notion of *possibility* and, in turn, think of 'cases' as such *possibilities*, we can treat 'true in a case' as 'possibly true' and get the following account of logical consequence—call it 'necessary consequence'.

- B is a *(necessary) consequence* of $A_1, \ldots, A_n$ if and only if there is no possibility in which $A_1, \ldots, A_n$ are all true but B is not true. (In other words, B is a consequence of $A_1, \ldots, A_n$ if and only if it is impossible for each given A_i to be true without B being true.)

Presumably, this account has it that, as above, 'Agnes is smart' is a consequence of (1) and (2). After all, presumably, it's not possible for (1) and (2) to be true without 'Agnes is smart' also being true. On the other hand, (7) is not a necessary consequence of (6), since, presumably, it is possible for (6) to be true without (7) being true.

Of course, taking 'cases' to be 'possibilities' requires some specification of what is possible, or at least some class of 'relevant possibilities'. The answer is not always straightforward. Is it possible to travel faster than the speed of light? Well, it's not *physically* possible (i.e., the physical laws prohibit it), but one might acknowledge a broader sense of 'possibility' in which such travel is possible—for example, *coherent* or *imaginable* or the like. If one restricts one's 'cases' to only physical possibilities, one gets a different account of logical consequence from an account that admits of possibilities that go beyond the physical laws.

In subsequent chapters, we will be exploring different logical theories of our language (or fragments of our language). A logical theory of our language (or a fragment thereof) is a theory that specifies the logical consequence relation over that language (or fragment). Some fragments of our language seem to call for some types of 'cases', while other fragments call for other (or additional) types. Subsequent chapters will clarify this point.

1.3 Valid arguments and truth

In general, theses require arguments. Consider the thesis that there are feline gods. Is the thesis true? An argument is required. Why think that there are feline gods? We need to examine the argument—the reasons that purport to 'support' the given thesis.

Arguments, for our purposes, comprise premises and a conclusion. The latter item is the thesis in question; the former purport to 'support' the conclusion. Arguments may be evaluated according to any relation of support (over sentences). An argument might be 'good' relative to some relation of support, but not good by another. For example, the argument from (6) to (7) is a good argument when assessed along the lines of (S1); however, it is not good when assessed in terms of (say) necessary consequence, since, as noted above, (7) is not a necessary consequence of (6).

In some areas of rational inquiry, empirical observation is often sufficient to figure out the truth. Suppose that you want to know whether there's a cat on the table. One reliable method is handy: look at the table and see whether there's a cat on it! Of course, 'real empirical science' is much more complicated than checking out cats, but empirical observation—empirical testing— is nonetheless a critical ingredient.

What about other pursuits for which there is little, if any, opportunity for settling matters by observation? Consider, for example, pure mathematics or philosophy. In such areas, theses cannot be empirically tested, at least in general. How, then, do we figure out the truth in such areas? Argument is the only recourse.

When argument is the only recourse, as in mathematics or (at least much of) philosophy, it makes sense to invoke the strictest relation of support—namely, logical consequence. Traditionally, an argument is said to be *valid*—strictly speaking, *logically valid*— if its conclusion is a logical consequence of its premises. We will follow suit.

Of course, a valid argument needn't be a proof of anything. After all, the 'definition' (or, for now, 'recipe') of *logical consequence* doesn't require that any of the premises be true. Rather, the given account requires only the *absence* of any 'counterexample', where these are defined as follows.

Definition 2. (Counterexample) *A counterexample to an argument is a case in which the premises are true but the conclusion is not true.*

We can say that B is a logical consequence of $A_1, \ldots, A_n$ if and only if there is no counterexample to the argument from (premises) $A_1, \ldots, A_n$ to (conclusion) B. In turn, an argument is *valid* just if there is no counterexample to it.

Accordingly, an argument may be valid—that is, its conclusion be a logical consequence of its premises—even though none of its premises are true. In mathematics and philosophy, validity is a necessary condition on suitable arguments; it is not sufficient. What is sufficient, for such pursuits, is a so-called *sound* argument.

Definition 3. (Sound Argument) *A sound argument is valid and all its premises are true.*

Suppose that, among the 'cases' in our definition of validity (or logical consequence), there is an 'actual case' @ such that A is true-in-@ just if A is true (i.e., actually true). On such an account, every sound argument has a true conclusion. After all, a sound argument, by definition, has all true premises. By supposition, a sentence is true just if true-in-@, and so all premises of a sound argument are true-in-@. But a sound argument, by definition, is also valid, and so, by definition, if its premises are true in a case, then so too is its conclusion. Since, as noted, the premises of any sound argument are true-in-@, so too is its conclusion.

Logic, in the end, serves the pursuit of truth; however, it does not principally concern itself with truth. Instead, logic, as above, has its chief concern with consequence—logical consequence. Logic aims to precisely specify valid arguments. Once the valid arguments are in order, rational inquiry may proceed to discern the sound arguments. For our purposes in this book, we will focus on different accounts of logical consequence, and some of the phenomena that motivate the various accounts.

1.4   Summary, looking ahead, and reading

Summary. Logical consequence is the chief concern of logic. An argument is *valid* just if its conclusion is a logical consequence of its premises. Logical consequence, in this book, will be understood as absence of counterexample, where a *counterexample* is a 'case' in which all the premises are true but the conclusion not true. One of the chief concerns of logic, broadly construed, is to figure out which 'cases' are involved in specifying the consequence relation on a given language (or fragment thereof). In subsequent chapters, we will look at different accounts of logical consequence—different logical theories of our language (or fragments thereof)—and some of the phenomena that have motivated them.

Looking Ahead. The next two chapters are devoted to stage-setting. Chapter 2 discusses features of language that are relevant to logic, and also discusses the general 'model-building' enterprise of formal logic. Chapter 3 briefly—and, for the most part, informally—introduces some useful set-theoretic notions. These two chapters will make subsequent discussion easier.

Further Reading. For related, accessible discussion of logic, see Read 1995, Haack 1978; Haack 1996. (And see the bibliographies therein for a host of other sources!) For a more advanced discussion of the 'recipe' of logical consequence, see Beall and Restall 2005.

Exercises

1. What is an argument?

2. What is a valid argument?

3. What is a sound argument?

4. What is the general 'recipe' for defining logical consequence (or validity)? What are the two key ingredients that one must specify in defining a consequence relation?

5. Consider the 'necessary consequence' relation, which takes cases to be possibilities. Assume, as is reasonable (!), that our actual world is possible—that is, that whatever is true (actually true) is possibly true. Question: on this account of logical consequence, are there any sound arguments that have false conclusions? If so, why? If not, why not?

6. As noted in the chapter, 'if and only if' (which is often abbreviated as 'iff') expresses two conditionals: 'A iff B' expresses both of the following conditionals.[3]

    - If A, then B.
    - If B, then A.

---

[3]Strictly speaking, what is expressed is the 'conjunction' of the two conditionals, but we leave the notion of *conjunctions* for the next chapter.

For our purposes, a biconditional '*A* iff *B*' is true so long as *A* and *B* are either both true or both false (and such biconditionals are false otherwise). With this in mind, consider the necessary consequence relation. Is the following argument valid (where, here, validity is necessary consequence)? If it is valid—if its conclusion is a necessary consequence of the premises—explain why it is valid. If not, explain why not.

(a) Max is happy if and only if Agnes is sleeping.
(b) Agnes is sleeping.
(c) Therefore, Max is happy.

What about the following argument?

(d) Max is happy if and only if Agnes is sleeping.
(e) Agnes is not sleeping.
(f) Therefore, Max is not happy.

7. Using the 'necessary consequence' account of validity, specify which of the following arguments are valid or invalid. Justify your answer.

   (a) Argument 1.
       i. If Agnes arrived at work on time, then her car worked properly.
       ii. If Agnes's car worked properly, then the car's ignition was not broken.
       iii. The car's ignition was not broken.
       iv. Therefore, Agnes arrived at work on time.

   (b) Argument 2.
       i. Either the sun will rise tomorrow or it will explode tomorrow.
       ii. The sun will not explode tomorrow.
       iii. Therefore, the sun will rise tomorrow.

   (c) Argument 3.
       i. If Max wins the lottery, then Max will be a millionaire.
       ii. Max will not win the lottery.
       iii. Therefore, Max will not be a millionaire.

(d) Argument 4.
  i. If Beetle is an extraterrestrial, then Beetle is not from earth.
  ii. Beetle is an extraterrestrial.
  iii. Therefore, Beetle is not from earth.

Sample answers

Answer 5. On the necessary-consequence sense of 'validity' (the sense in question), an argument is *valid* iff every possibility (e.g., possible circumstance) in which the premises are all true is one in which the conclusion is true. Hence, if the actual world—the 'real' world, the way things really are—counts as a possibility, then it itself cannot be a case in which the premises of a valid argument are true but the conclusion false. But, then, any *sound* argument—that is, a valid argument whose premises are all (actually) true—is one in which the conclusion is true, and so not false.[4]

Answer 6. The argument from (6a) and (6b) to (6c) is valid in the necessary-consequence approach to validity: it is not possible for both of (6a) and (6b) to be true without (6c) being true. After all, recall that (6a) expresses not only that *if Max is happy then Agnes is sleeping*; it also expresses that *if Agnes is sleeping then Max is happy*. Now, consider any possibility (and possible circumstance) in which both (6a) and (6b) are true, that is, a possible circumstance in which not only Agnes is sleeping, but *if Agnes is sleeping (in that circumstance), then Max is happy (in that circumstance)*. Well, then, no matter what possible circumstance we choose, it'll be one in which Max is happy if it's one in which both (6a) and (6b) are true. (Of course, there are, presumably, many possibilities in which neither (6a) nor (6b) are true, but this does not affect the necessary-consequence sense in which the given argument is valid. Why?)

---

[4]This last step—from *true* to *not false*—is something that some logical theories reject, but these theories are left for later chapters.

2

Language, Form, and Logical Theories

*Traditionally, (formal) logic is concerned with
the analysis of sentences... and of proof...
with attention to the* form *in abstraction from the* matter.
– Alonzo Church (1956)

The aim of this chapter is to cover three topics: features of language that are relevant to logic; the aim of 'formal languages' with respect to modern logic; and the idea of rivalry among logical theories. Subsequent chapters, following the brief 'set-theoretic toolbox' in Chapter 3, look at different logical theories and phenomena that motivate them. This chapter, like its predecessor, remains abstract; its aim is simply to lay out some big-picture ideas that will be useful for subsequent discussion.

2.1 Language

Languages have a syntax and semantics. The *semantics* of a language involves the meanings of its parts. One cannot have semantics (whatever, exactly, semantics may be) without first having *sentences*. That's where so-called syntax enters. Syntax provides the uninterpreted sentences of a language, while semantics does the work of providing meaning. For our purposes, a *syntax* provides

- *syntactic ingredients*—basic building blocks of the language;
- a set of (well-formed) *sentences* of the language.

The set of syntactic ingredients contains all of the items involved in the given language's sentences. Consider, for example, the following sentence of English.

Agnes is sleeping.

There are various syntactic ingredients used in this sentence. To begin, there are the individual letters 'A', 'g', 'n', and so on.

Such letters are ingredients for other ingredients, in particular, the name 'Agnes' and the predicate 'is sleeping' (which is spelled with an invisible letter called 'space', which falls between the two occurrences of 's' in 'is sleeping'). Finally, there is a punctuation mark, namely, '.'. These syntactic ingredients are put together in the appropriate way to form the given sentence, namely, 'Agnes is sleeping.'.

What if we took the above ingredients (e.g., the name 'Agnes' and predicate 'is sleeping') and put them together as follows?

is sleeping. Agnes

Is this a sentence of English? No. The given string of ingredients is not among English's set of *sentences*. Of course, it's conceivable that English could've evolved in such a way that 'is sleeping. Agnes' counted as a sentence; however, English's actual syntax—in particular, its grammar—doesn't count the given string as an English sentence.

For our purposes, one may think of a language's syntax as specifying which of its many strings of ingredients count as sentences of the language.

What about the *semantics* of a language? As above, a language's semantics has to do with the meanings of its parts. For present purposes, we may think of semantics in a rather limited sense: namely, whatever is involved in the 'truth conditions' of a sentence—the conditions under which a sentence is true. In effect, providing truth conditions for the sentences of a language amounts to filling in the two ingredients involved in the 'recipe' for logical consequence (see Chapter 1)—namely, *cases* and *truth in a case*.

Consider an example from the language *Enilef* (pronounced 'En-ill-ef', with accent on 'En').[1] Among the predicates of Enilef is 'mew eow'. Among the names in Enilef is 'Senga'. The question is: under what conditions is 'Senga mew eow' true? What, in other words, does it take for 'Senga mew eow' to be true? Here is a natural thought:

- 'Senga mew eow' is true if and only if the referent of 'Senga' has the property expressed by 'mew eow'.

---

[1] This is a made-up language.

How do we generalize this to the idea of *truth in a case*? We first need to have some idea of what these 'cases' are.

For now, we will skip details and think of cases as 'possible circumstances' along familiar—though, admittedly, imprecise—lines. (E.g., there's a possible circumstance in which 'Logic: The Basics' refers to a book other than the one you're reading. There's a possible circumstance in which 'is a cat' expresses the property of *being a horse*. And so on.) Letting c be any such 'possible circumstance', we can generalize the condition above to get an example of truth-in-a-case conditions.

- 'Senga mew eow' is true in a possible circumstance c if and only if the referent of 'Senga' in c has the property expressed by 'mew eow' in c.

Pending further details about the 'nature' of c (the nature of our 'possible circumstances'), the above account is an example of truth conditions or, more relevantly, truth-in-a-case conditions.

We will return to this topic in subsequent chapters, where the interaction between truth-in-a-case conditions and logical consequence will be clearer. For now, one may think of 'semantics' as above: whatever is involved in the truth conditions of sentences.

2.2   Atoms, connectives, and molecules

Chemistry recognizes a distinction between atoms and molecules. Atoms, at least in the original sense of the term, contain no parts (other than themselves). Molecules, on the other hand, are composed of atoms. Molecules are what you get by connecting atoms together.

Language likewise admits of atoms and molecules, in particular, *atomic sentences* and *molecular sentences*. Consider, for example, the following sentences.

1. Max is running.
2. Agnes is running.
3. Max likes beans.
4. Agnes likes beans.

Typically, logicians treat (1)–(4) as *atomic*. For purposes of logic (or, at least, many standard logical theories), (1)–(4) have no significant 'logical parts'. Such sentences are simple, subject-predicate sentences. Unless the given predicates (or, perhaps, names) are thought to carry special logical significance, the sentences are treated as basic atomics.

The distinction between atomics and molecular sentences, at least in logic, turns on the idea of *logical connectives*, which are a species of so-called *sentential connectives*.[2] Sentential connectives take sentences and make new (bigger) sentences. Sentential connectives have a 'degree' or 'arity', which marks the number of sentences a given connective requires in order to make a new sentence. Among commonly recognized connectives in English are the following.

- Conjunction: ... *and* ...
- Disjunction:[3] ... *or* ... (or both)
- Negation: *It is not true that* ...

The first two are *binary* connectives; they take two (not necessarily distinct) sentences to make a new sentence. For example, if we plug (1) and (2) into the slots for 'and', we get the *conjunction* of (1) and (2), namely,

5. Max is running and Agnes is running.

Similarly, if we plug (3) and (4) into the slots in 'or', we get

6. Max likes beans or Agnes likes beans (or both).

Unlike conjunction and disjunction, negation is a *unary* connective; it takes exactly one sentence to make a new sentence, namely, the *negation* of the given sentence. For example, the negations of (1)–(4) are as follows.

7. It is not true that Max is running.

8. It is not true that Agnes is running.

9. It is not true that Max likes beans.

10. It is not true that Agnes like beans.

---

[2] This is slightly narrow, but for present purposes will suffice. The broader category of 'logical expressions' is more accurate. We will return to this topic when we discuss Identity in Chapter 8.

[3] This connective is called *inclusive disjunction*, which is different from its relative *exclusive disjunction*, which is '... or ... (but not both)'.

Note that, in English, negation is also expressed when it appears 'inside' of sentences; it needn't take its august form at the beginning of sentences. For example, the following are equivalent to (7)–(10): they too are the negations of (1)–(4).

11. Max is not running.
12. Agnes is not running.
13. Max does not like beans.
14. Agnes does not like beans.

With some sense of connectives in mind, we can now officially define what it is to be an atomic sentence of a language, and similarly a molecular sentence of a language. For our purposes, every language has some set of sentential connectives, and so we assume as much in the following definitions.[4] We will let $\mathcal{L}$ be an arbitrary language (e.g., English or whathaveyou), and A be any sentence of $\mathcal{L}$.

Definition 4. (Atomic Sentence) *A is an atomic sentence of language $\mathcal{L}$ if and only if A contains none of $\mathcal{L}$'s connectives.*

Definition 5. (Molecular Sentence) *A is a molecular sentence of language $\mathcal{L}$ if and only if A contains one or more of $\mathcal{L}$'s connectives.*

2.3   Connectives and form

With the idea of connectives comes the idea of *form*—in particular, *logical form*.[5] Each language has a set of connectives. In doing logic, logicians traditionally focus on some subset of a language's connectives, namely, the ones that are deemed to be *logically significant*. Such connectives are called *logical connectives*; they are the ones in virtue of which 'logical form' is usually defined.

To get an idea of 'logical form', consider again some of the molecular sentences mentioned above, say, (5). This sentence is

---

[4]What makes a connective a *logical* connective is a topic to which we *briefly* turn in §2.4 below. We will not discuss the philosophically challenging issue of what, exactly, makes a connective a logical connective.

[5]There are ongoing debates about what, exactly, logical form amounts to. Given the aims of this book, the current discussion simplifies the situation a great deal, sidestepping many such issues.

a conjunction of two atomic sentences, namely, (1) and (2); however, we could've used our conjunction (our connective) to form the conjunction of *any* two sentences.

For convenience, let us use the symbol '∧' for conjunction. In turn, letting A and B be any two sentences, we can say that conjunctions have the following logical form.

$$A \land B$$

This isn't to say that every conjunction has the syntactic form $A \land B$. Quite often, conjunctions have a different surface form. (Consider, e.g., 'Max and Agnes like beans', which is a convenient way of expressing the conjunction 'Max likes beans and Agnes likes beans'.) When we talk about *form*, we mean *logical form*, which is a syntactic 'form' relevant to logic.

Of course, a conjunction might have a more illuminating form if one digs a bit deeper into the given conjuncts.[6] To see this, let us use '∨' for disjunction, and also use '¬' for negation. Now, consider the *conjunction* of (4) and (6). This is still a conjunction, but its particular form is illuminated by the following.

$$A \land (B \lor A)$$

In this case, conjunction is the 'main connective', but instead of taking two atomics conjunction is now conjoining an atomic (viz., (4)) and a molecular sentence (viz., (6)).

Similarly, consider the disjunction of (1) and (7). Since (7) is the negation of (1), its form—letting A represent (1)—is simply $\neg A$. In turn, the disjunction of (1) and (7) has the following form.

$$A \lor \neg A$$

You can consider other examples involving the three given connectives.

2.4   Validity and form

Logical consequence (or validity), as in Chapter 1, is absence of counterexample: B is a logical consequence of A just if there's

---

[6]The *conjuncts* of a conjunction are the sentences that are conjoined by conjunction: A and B are the conjuncts of the conjunction $A \land B$.

no counterexample to the argument from A to B, that is, just if there's no 'case' in which A is true but B not true. In contemporary logic (but also in much of traditional logic), a further feature of logical consequence is highlighted: *logical form*. Many standard logical theories maintain that validity is essentially tied to 'form'. In particular, the idea is that the validity of an argument is at least partially in virtue of form.

Sentences, as above, have logical forms. Arguments, in turn, immediately enjoy logical forms. After all, arguments, which are (ordered) sets of sentences, have a logical form that derives from the form of its constituent sentences. For example, consider the argument from premises (1) and (2) to conclusion (5). (The word 'Therefore' is inserted to mark the conclusion of the given argument; it isn't really part of the argument.)

1. Max is running.
2. Agnes is running.
5. Therefore, Max is running and Agnes is running.

We can abstract away from the particular content of the above argument to get the following *logical form* of the argument— sometimes called *argument form*. Here, we use 'P' and 'C' to mark premises and conclusion; they are not really part of the given argument form.

P. A
P. B
C. $A \wedge B$

By using a comma to separate premises, and using '$\therefore$' to separate the premises from the conclusion, we can conveniently display the above argument form thus: $A, B \therefore A \wedge B$.[7]

Similarly, the argument from premises (6) and (9) to conclusion (4) has the following argument form: $A \vee B, \neg A \therefore B$.

Why bother thinking about argument forms? As above, logical consequence, according to standard thinking, has something to

---

[7]Note well: '$\therefore$' is used as a convenient way of representing an argument or argument form (separating premises from conclusion in the given form); we don't use '$\mathcal{X} \therefore A$' to *say* anything. Still, if you'd like to pronounce '$\therefore$', you can use its standard pronunciation 'therefore'. (Again, though, the symbol is not being used to *say* anything, but just to represent argument forms.)

do with logical form. In particular, the validity of an argument is often thought to be at least partly due to its logical form. For example, consider, again, the following form: $A, B \therefore A \wedge B$. Regardless of what sentences you plug into 'A' or 'B', you wind up with a valid argument—at least according to standard logical theories. For example, let our 'cases', once again, be something like 'possible circumstances'. Is there any possible circumstance in which both of A and B are true but their conjunction $A \wedge B$ is not true? On brief reflection, it is difficult to conceive of such a case, at least if $\wedge$ is understood as standard conjunction. To make this plain, we can consider the natural 'truth conditions' for conjunctions. A natural approach to the truth conditions for conjunction goes as follows.[8]

- A conjunction $A \wedge B$ is true-in-a-possible-circumstance-c if and only if A is true-in-c and B is also true-in-c.

Pending further details about our given cases c, this 'truth condition' (i.e., *truth-in-a-case-c* condition) ensures that any argument of the form $A, B \therefore A \wedge B$ is valid. After all, an argument is valid if and only if it is without counterexample; it is without counterexample iff there is no case in which the premises are true but the conclusion not true. Can there be a case in which A and B are both true but $A \wedge B$ is not true? The truth condition above answers the question. According to the given truth condition, if A and B are both true-in-*some given case* c, then $A \wedge B$ is true-in-c too. Hence, given the above truth condition, there cannot be a case in which both A and B are true but $A \wedge B$ is not true. Whence, the given argument form, namely $A, B \therefore A \wedge B$, is valid—at least given the above truth condition for conjunction.

2.5   Language and formal languages

Today, the discipline of logic is largely *formal logic*. In part, formal logic is so called because it often aims to specify valid argument *forms*, and it sees logical consequence as being largely a matter of such forms. Formal logic is also so called for another reason: namely, that contemporary logicians almost always

---

[8]Strictly speaking, we are giving *truth-in-a-case-c* conditions, but it is cumbersome to always write this, and so sometimes we use 'truth conditions' as shorthand for *truth-in-a-case* conditions.

construct 'formal languages' in their aim to specify logical consequence. Formal languages serve as idealized, heuristic models of a given natural language (or fragment thereof); they are intended to illuminate the behavior of logical connectives and, ultimately, the target consequence relation.

Logic, in the first instance, is about what follows from what in a given *natural language* (or some fragment thereof). Natural languages are familiar languages like English, Spanish, French, German, Polish, Mandarin, and so on. Natural languages are powerful and useful tools; however, they are also rife with features such as ambiguity and vagueness. Such features, while perhaps partly contributing to the flexibility of natural languages, can be distracting if one is trying to clearly, precisely specify the logic—that is, logical consequence relation—of the given language. In large part, this is why logicians construct 'artificial languages' to help with the task. The situation is familiar from science. Physicists aim to illuminate the real but messy physical world. To achieve clarity and precision, physicists abstract away from the messiness; they use idealized models of reality. Similarly, modern logicians construct precise, artificial languages to model our 'real language'. Recourse to artificial languages helps avoid otherwise distracting features of the target, real language.

To some extent, we have already employed artificial symbols in an effort to achieve clarity. The use of such ad hoc symbols doesn't make for an artificial language, but the idea is similar. Artificial languages, like natural languages, have a syntax and semantics. Unlike the case of natural languages, artificial languages are very precise, with the syntax being rigorously defined and the semantics being precisely, mathematically defined. Indeed, the semantics of artificial languages is often called *formal semantics*. Usually, such 'semantics' provides little more than what is required for specifying 'truth conditions' (or, more accurately, *truth-in-a-case conditions*), as above.

We will see examples of artificial languages in subsequent chapters. For now, we turn to the idea of 'rivalry' among logical theories.

2.6 Logical theories: rivalry

It is generally thought that each natural language, on the whole, has exactly one consequence relation—or, in short, one logic. Assuming as much, the aim of a *logical theory* is to specify the logic of a given language. In doing so, a logical theory aims to clearly record all of the valid argument forms of the given language. With respect to English, for example, the aim of a logical theory is to specify English's consequence relation, to specify the valid argument forms of English.

Scientific theories—or theological theories, or psychological theories, or etc.—often disagree about a given phenomenon. In such cases, the theories are said to be 'rival theories' of the given phenomenon. For example, one scientific theory might say that the earth revolves around the sun, while another might say that the sun revolves around the earth. The two theories give rival accounts of the same phenomenon—the sun's rising (as it were).

Can there be rivalry among logical theories? Yes. Not only can there be rivalry among logical theories; there *is* rivalry among logical theories. Subsequent chapters will discuss rival logical theories. For now, it is worth briefly clarifying two common ways in which logical theories might be rivals.

Logical theories, for our purposes, are always theories about the consequence relation of a particular language (or fragment thereof). We will say that logical theories cannot be rivals unless they are theories of the same language (or the same fragment of some language). Two common ways in which logical theories may be rivals are as follows, but will only be illustrated in subsequent chapters.

- Different Logical Connectives: suppose that two theories aim to specify the logical consequence relation of some (natural) language $\mathcal{L}$. The theories might be rivals by disagreeing about $\mathcal{L}$'s set of logical connectives. (E.g., both theories might say that 'and' is a sentential connective of $\mathcal{L}$, but the theories might disagree as to whether the given connective should be counted as properly *logical*, that is, whether 'and' plays any logically significant role in valid arguments.)

- Different Logical Behavior: suppose that two theories aim to specify the logical consequence relation of some (natural) language $\mathcal{L}$. Suppose, further, that both theories agree on which of $\mathcal{L}$'s connectives count as properly *logical* connectives. The theories might nonetheless be rivals by disagreeing about the *logical behavior* of the given connectives. (E.g., one theory might say that $\neg\neg A \therefore A$ is a valid form in $\mathcal{L}$, while the other theory disagrees by saying that some instances of the given argument form have counterexamples.)

For the most part, this book will only cover the second route towards logical rivalry.

Summary, looking ahead, and reading

Summary. Languages have a syntax and semantics. Syntax provides the basic ingredients of the language, and in particular a set of (uninterpreted) sentences. Semantics provides whatever is required for 'truth conditions' of all sentences of the language. Sentences have *logical forms*. Arguments, being (ordered) sets of sentences, likewise have logical forms—argument forms. Validity is often thought to be at least partly due to the logical form of arguments. Logic, qua discipline, aims to specify all valid forms of a given language (or fragment thereof). For convenience and clarity, artificial languages are constructed to illustrate the logical forms of a given language. Logical theories give an account of the logical consequence relation of some given language. Rival logical theories disagree about the behavior of logical connectives (or disagree about which connectives count as logical). In subsequent chapters, we will look at rival logical theories, or at least the general idea involved in some such rivals.

Looking Ahead. The next chapter discusses a few basic set-theoreti tools. We will use such tools to talk about various logical theories in succeeding chapters.

Further Reading. For an accessible, related, but more involved discussion of this chapter's various themes, see Sainsbury 2001 and Read 1995, and also the highly classic 'Introduction' in Church 1956. (Also see bibliographies therein!)

Exercises

1. What is a sentential connective? What is a unary connective? What is a binary connective? (What is the degree or

arity of a sentential connective?)

2. Relying on the informal idea of 'possible circumstance' for our 'cases', and using the 'truth condition' in §2.4 for conjunction, say whether the following argument form is valid: $A \wedge B \therefore B$. Justify your answer by invoking the general definition of 'validity' (or logical consequence) and the given truth condition.

3. In §2.4 we gave a natural truth condition for conjunction. Give what you'd take to be a natural 'truth condition' (strictly, *truth-in-a-case* condition) for disjunction. Do the same for negation. (You'll need these conditions in some of what follows.)

4. Consider the argument from premises (6) and (9) to conclusion (4). Using the symbolism introduced above, give its argument form. Taking 'cases' to be 'possible circumstances', and using the truth conditions that you provided for disjunction and negation (and, if need be, the condition in §2.4 for conjunction), is the given form valid? Justify your answer.

5. Consider the argument form $\neg A \vee B, A \therefore B$. Taking 'cases' to be 'possible circumstances', and using the truth conditions that you provided for disjunction and negation, is the given form valid? Justify your answer. (Your answer may turn, in part, on your philosophy of 'possible circumstances'!)

6. Let us say that a *sentence* is *logically true* if and only if there is no case in which it is not true. Using the truth conditions that you gave for disjunction and negation, say whether the disjunction of (2) and (8) is logically true. Justify your answer. (Also, what is the logical form of the given sentence? Is it true that, given your truth conditions, *every* sentence of that form is logically true?)

7. Consider the following argument.
   (a) Max is a bachelor.
   (b) Therefore, Max is unmarried.

   Neither sentence has any of our given connectives, and so both sentences are atomic, at least according to our definitions above. As such, atomics have no significant logical form. Instead, following the policy according to which distinct sentences are represented by distinct letters,[9] we would represent the argument form thus: $A \therefore B$. Is this argument form *valid*? If so, why? If not, why not? If there's not enough information to tell, what is the missing information? What premise might be added to make the argument valid?

8. Consider, again, the argument above from 'Max is a bachelor' to 'Max is unmarried'. Is the conclusion a *necessary consequence* of the premise? If so, what, if anything, does this suggest about the role of 'logical form' in the 'necessary consequence' account of validity given in Chapter 1?

9. In your own words, say what it is to give *truth-in-a-case conditions* (or, for our purposes, truth conditions) for sentences. Why, if at all, is this activity—that is, giving so-called truth conditions—essential to an account of *logical consequence* as we've defined it (in Chapter 1)?

Sample answers

Answer 2. On the current 'possible circumstance' approach to cases, the argument form $A \wedge B \therefore B$ is valid iff there's no possible circumstance in which $A \wedge B$ is true but B not true (for any sentences A and B). On this account of validity, $A \wedge B \therefore B$ is valid. Proof: suppose that c is a possible circumstance in which $A \wedge B$ is true. By the (given) truth conditions for conjunction (see §2.4), if $A \wedge B$ is true-in-c then both A and B are true-in-c, and so B is true-in-c. But, by supposition, $A \wedge B$ *is* true-in-c, and so we conclude that B is true-in-c too. Hence, since what we've said about c applies to *any* possible circumstance, we conclude that there can't be any possible circumstance in which $A \wedge B$ is true but B not true; and, so, there can't be a counterexample to the given argument form.

Answer 3. Here are natural truth conditions (i.e., more accurately, truth-in-a-case conditions) for disjunction and negation.

- A disjunction $A \vee B$ is true-in-a-possible-circumstance-c if and only if A is true-in-c or B is true-in-c (or both).

---

[9]This is the policy that we will generally follow.

- A negation $\neg A$ is true-in-a-possible-circumstance-c if and only if A is false-in-c.

3

Set-theoretic Tools

Sets are among the most useful things you'll never see.
– Me

This chapter introduces a few set-theoretic tools. We are *not* going to discuss a full set theory (i.e., a full theory of *sets*), but rather only get acquainted with some of the ideas. The aim is to acquire a few useful tools for subsequent chapters.

3.1 Sets

For our purposes, a *set* is any 'collection' of 'things'. Scare quotes are used around the words 'collection' and 'things' to flag that these words are used in a way that might slightly deviate from ordinary usage. In particular, a *thing*, in effect, is whatever exists or even possibly exists; it needn't be—although it can be—some concrete object like a tree or cat or person. In effect, anything you can talk about is a thing in the target sense.[1] Moreover, a *collection*, in the relevant sense, needn't be the result of anyone's actually collecting things together. For our purposes, a collection of things can exist even if nobody has—or will, or could—collect the given things together. For example, we can acknowledge the collection of all things that nobody will ever collect together!

3.1.1 *Members*

The things that are *in* a set are called its *members* or *elements*. We will use '∈' as our binary predicate for the binary membership relation, that is, the relation . . . *is a member of* . . . For example, if a is a member of set $\mathcal{X}$, we will write '$a \in \mathcal{X}$' to say as much.

---

[1]Question: can you talk about a square circle? (This question is posed only to flag that our account of 'things' may not be ideal, but it'll do for present purposes.)

3.1.2   *Abstraction and Membership*

We will use brace notation to name sets. For example, $\{2,4,6,8\}$ is the set containing 2, 4, 6, and 8.

We named $\{2,4,6,8\}$ by listing its members and employing the brace notation. This works so long as we have only finitely many members, but is only convenient when we have a very small handful of members. Accordingly, we will make use of a much more powerful way of naming sets, namely, 'definition by abstraction'. Consider the English predicate '... is a cat'. *Definition by abstraction* allows us to name the set of all (and only) cats by writing '$\{x : x$ is a cat$\}$', which may be read 'the set of all x such that x is a cat'. Similarly, one can name the set of all cats bigger than Agnes by writing

$$\{x : x \text{ is a cat and } x \text{ is bigger than Agnes}\}$$

which, as above, is the set of all x such that x is a cat and x is bigger than Agnes.

Think of each set as having an *entry condition*, which is the condition that is both *necessary and sufficient* for being a member of the given set. On this way of talking, *being a cat* is the entry condition for $\{x : x$ is a cat$\}$. In general, '...' is the entry condition for $\{x : x$ is ...$\}$, which is the set of all x that satisfy the given entry condition. Accordingly, for our purposes, the *criterion of membership*—what it takes to be a member of a set—is the following so-called *comprehension principle* (sometimes axiom).[2]

Definition 6. (Membership Criterion) $x \in \{y : \ldots\}$ *iff x satisfies condition* ...

In other words, something x is in $\{y : \ldots\}$ if and only if x satisfies the given entry condition. For example, consider, again, the set $\{x : x$ is a cat$\}$, which is the set of all x such that x is a cat (i.e., the set of all cats). Our criterion of membership tells us that Agnes is a member of $\{x : x$ is a cat$\}$ if and only if Agnes is a cat.

---

[2]Bertrand Russell showed that, at least in classical set theory, not all predicates can serve as entry conditions, that is, that not any old predicate determines a set. (To see Russell's point, consider the predicate 'x is not a member of x'.)

Putting definition by abstraction and comprehension together, consider our previous example, namely, $\{2, 4, 6, 8\}$. If we let 'Fx' abbreviate 'x is an even positive integer strictly less than 10',[3] then we can give another name of $\{2, 4, 6, 8\}$ via set abstraction by using '$\{x : Fx\}$'. Comprehension, in turn, tells us that something y (no matter what it is) is a member of $\{x : Fx\}$ iff 'Fx' is true of y, that is, that $y \in \{x : Fx\}$ iff y is an even positive integer strictly less than ten.

3.1.3 *Criterion of identity*

In order to know whether two sets are the *same set*, we need what philosophers call a *criterion of identity*, something that precisely individuates sets—something that tells us whether set $\mathcal{X}$ counts as the same set as set $\mathcal{Y}$. The criterion we will use—and the criterion used in contemporary set theory—is the so-called principle of extensionality, which is as follows. We will use '$=$' as our binary predicate for *. . . is the same (set) as. . . .*[4] Accordingly, if $\mathcal{X}$ and $\mathcal{Y}$ are the same set, then we express as much by writing '$\mathcal{X} = \mathcal{Y}$'. The *principle of extensionality* is:

Definition 7. (Identity Criterion for Sets; Extensionality) $\mathcal{X} = \mathcal{Y}$ *if and only if $\mathcal{X}$ and $\mathcal{Y}$ have exactly the same members.*

In other words, *same members* is all that matters for the 'identity' of sets. Accordingly, it doesn't matter *how* you specify them; so long as they have precisely the same members, the specified sets are the same. Hence, the set of all even prime numbers is exactly the same set as the set containing Max's favorite number, and the same as the set containing only the sum of 1 and 1, namely, $\{2\}$. Similarly, $\{1, 1, 2, 1\} = \{1, 2\}$ since there's no member of the one set that isn't a member of the other. (True, some members 'appear' more than once, but the criterion of identity says that that doesn't matter.)

---

[3]It is customary in modern logic to put a predicate before the subject term(s), and we will follow suit.

[4]We will also use this symbol for *identity*, in general, but no serious confusion should arise.

3.1.4 *The empty set*

Notice that we have an empty set, that is, a set containing no members. After all, consider the set $\{x : x \neq x\}$, which is the set of all x such that x is not identical to itself. Is there anything that satisfies the entry condition '$x \neq x$'? No; everything is identical to itself. Hence, nothing is in $\{x : x \neq x\}$. We have an empty set!

By our criterion of identity, two sets are the same just if they have the members. Hence, if $\mathcal{X}$ has *no* members, and $\mathcal{Y}$ has *no* members, then $\mathcal{X}$ is the same set as $\mathcal{Y}$. Accordingly, we can have only one empty set—that is, a set with no members—and, since we have at least one, we can give it a special (and standard) name, namely '$\emptyset$'. So, $\emptyset$ is *the* set such that $x \notin \emptyset$ for all x.

3.1.5 *Other sets: sets out of sets*

Once we have some sets, we can form new sets by using a few so-called operations on sets (or set-forming operations).[5] There are a variety of standard such operations, but we need mention only a few: union and intersection. We define these operations as follows.

Definition 8. (Union) *The union of $\mathcal{X}$ and $\mathcal{Y}$ is named '$\mathcal{X} \cup \mathcal{Y}$' and defined thus:* $\mathcal{X} \cup \mathcal{Y} = \{x : x \in \mathcal{X} \text{ or } x \in \mathcal{Y}\}$.

Definition 9. (Intersection) *The intersection of $\mathcal{X}$ and $\mathcal{Y}$ is named '$\mathcal{X} \cap \mathcal{Y}$' and defined thus:* $\mathcal{X} \cap \mathcal{Y} = \{x : x \in \mathcal{X} \text{ and } x \in \mathcal{Y}\}$.

Though, in this book, this terminology (union, intersection) is not explicitly used a lot, it is useful to have in mind.

3.1.6 *A few important relations among sets*

An important relation between sets is called the *subset* relation, which is standardly symbolized with '$\subseteq$', and defined as follows.

Definition 10. (Subset) $\mathcal{X} \subseteq \mathcal{Y}$ *iff everything in $\mathcal{X}$ is in $\mathcal{Y}$. (Equivalently: there is nothing in $\mathcal{X}$ that is not in $\mathcal{Y}$.)*

Given this definition, every set is a subset of itself. (After all, if $\mathcal{X}$ is a set, then everything in $\mathcal{X}$ is in $\mathcal{X}$!) So, for example, the (non-empty) subsets of $\{a, b\}$ are $\{a\}, \{b\}$, and $\{a, b\}$ itself.[6]

---

[5]This section can be skipped until Chapter 8.

[6]It turns out that $\emptyset$ is a subset of any set. After all, let $\mathcal{Y}$ be any set. Since there's nothing in $\emptyset$, there's nothing in $\emptyset$ that's not in $\mathcal{Y}$!

A closely related relation is so-called *proper subsethood*, which is defined thus:

Definition 11. (Proper Subset) $\mathcal{X} \subset \mathcal{Y}$ *iff* $\mathcal{X} \subseteq \mathcal{Y}$ *and there's something in* $\mathcal{Y}$ *that is not in* $\mathcal{X}$.

Both of these relations among sets are important throughout the book.

3.2   Ordered sets: pairs and n-tuples

One of our goals, in learning a bit about sets, is to get a handle on *functions*. To understand functions, we need to understand *relations*. To understand *relations*, at least in a set-theoretic framework, we need to understand the idea of *ordered pairs* and, in general, *ordered n-tuples*. That's what we'll do in this section, and then move to relations and, in turn, functions in the next few sections.

Recall that, by our criterion of identity, two sets are identical iff they have the same members. Hence, as above, $\{1, 1, 2, 1\} = \{1, 2\}$, as there's no member of the former set that's not in the latter set, and no member of the latter set that's not in the former set. Our criterion of identity doesn't care how many times a member appears in a set, or in what order a member appears; indeed, as far as *sets* go, our criterion of identity ignores any structure among the elements—it treats sets as, in some sense, structureless entities, entities that are individuated not by any structure among members but, rather, only by the identity of the members.

For a variety of reasons, we often want to consider 'collections' where the *structure* or *order* of elements matters. In other words, we have reason to acknowledge 'collections' that, while being the same with respect to members (and, hence, the same *sets*), ought to count as different entities because the *order* of elements differs. For example, in Euclidean geometry one thinks of points as being *ordered pairs*, where x is the first coordinate (marking the place on the x-axis) and y the second coordinate (marking the place on the y-axis). Clearly, $\{1, 2\}$ cannot serve as an ordered pair in geometry, since $\{1, 2\}$ is the same as $\{2, 1\}$.

We can think of *ordered pairs* as sets that have a stricter criterion of identity than extensionality (see Def. 7). In particular, the identity of an ordered pair is determined by *two* factors: the identity of the elements (as before), and the *order* of the elements. This is different from our sets, where identity turns entirely on the one factor, namely, identity of elements. Using angle notation for ordered pairs, where $\langle x, y \rangle$ is the ordered pair whose first coordinate is x and second coordinate y, we give the following identity criterion for ordered pairs.

Definition 12. (Ordered Pairs) $\langle w, x \rangle = \langle y, z \rangle$ *if and only if* $w = y$ *and* $x = z$.

Hence, while $\{1, 2\} = \{2, 1\}$, the case is different for the ordered pairs: $\langle 1, 2 \rangle \neq \langle 2, 1 \rangle$, since we don't have it that $1 = 2$ and $2 = 1$.

Generalizing we can use our ordered pairs to define ordered n-tuples (e.g., triples, quadruples, quintuples, etc.) as follows.[7]

Definition 13. (Ordered n-tuples) *An ordered n-tuple* $\langle x_1, \ldots, x_n \rangle$ *is the ordered pair* $\langle \langle x_1, \ldots, x_{n-1} \rangle, x_n \rangle$.

So, an ordered triple of x, y, and z (in that order) will be $\langle \langle x, y \rangle, z \rangle$. For example, the ordered triple of 1, 2, and 3 (in that order) is $\langle \langle 1, 2 \rangle, 3 \rangle$. Similarly, an ordered quadruple $\langle w, x, y, z \rangle$ is the ordered pair whose first coordinate is the ordered triple $\langle w, x, y \rangle$ and second coordinate z. For convenience, we also allow for 'ordered 1-tuples', and identify $\langle x \rangle$ with x itself.

« *Parenthetical remark.* You might be wondering whether, in order to accommodate ordered pairs, we really need to admit entirely new entities in addition to our original sets. Are there already (unordered) sets that sufficiently play the role of ordered pairs? The answer, due to mathematician Kazimierz Kuratowski, is affirmative: we don't need to acknowledge new entities; our old sets do the trick. In particular, define $\langle x, y \rangle$ to be $\{\{x\}, \{x, y\}\}$. In turn, one can prove that $\{\{w\}, \{w, x\}\} = \{\{y\}, \{y, z\}\}$ iff $w = y$ and $x = z$, thereby showing that our ordinary (unordered) set

---

[7]A related and equally good approach to ordered n-tuples constructs them in the reverse order from that below: viz., taking ordered n-tuples of $\langle x_1, \ldots, x_n \rangle$ to be $\langle x_1, \langle x_2, \ldots, x_n \rangle \rangle$. An heuristic surface advantage of our officially adopted approach in Def. 13 is that it corresponds to the familiar way of thinking of n-ary functions where the input (viz., an n-tuple) comes first and the output second.

$\{\{x\}, \{x, y\}\}$ plays the role of an ordered pair; the given (unordered) set has the target identity criterion (see Def. 12). *End parenthetical.* »

3.2.1 *Cartesian Product*

Now that we have the notion of an *ordered set*, we can introduce a useful operation on sets, that is, something that takes sets and produces sets. The operation in question is the *product* operation, which is defined as follows for any sets $\mathcal{X}$ and $\mathcal{Y}$.

Definition 14. (Cartesian Product) *The* product *of* $\mathcal{X}$ *and* $\mathcal{Y}$ *is* $\mathcal{X} \times \mathcal{Y}$, *which is defined to be* $\{\langle x, y \rangle : x \in \mathcal{X} \text{ and } y \in \mathcal{Y}\}$. *Hence,* $\mathcal{X} \times \mathcal{Y}$ *contains all ordered pairs* $\langle x, y \rangle$ *such that the first coordinate is in* $\mathcal{X}$ *and the second coordinate in* $\mathcal{Y}$.

So, the product of sets $\mathcal{X}$ and $\mathcal{Y}$ is a set of ordered pairs, namely, the set of all pairs that you get by taking the first element from $\mathcal{X}$ and the second from $\mathcal{Y}$. For example, let $\mathcal{X} = \{1, 2\}$ and $\mathcal{Y} = \{2, 3\}$. In this case, the product of $\mathcal{X}$ and $\mathcal{Y}$, namely, $\mathcal{X} \times \mathcal{Y}$, is $\{\langle 1, 2 \rangle, \langle 1, 3 \rangle, \langle 2, 2 \rangle, \langle 2, 3 \rangle\}$. Similarly, $\mathcal{X} \times \mathcal{X}$ and $\mathcal{Y} \times \mathcal{Y}$ are $\{\langle 1, 1 \rangle, \langle 1, 2 \rangle, \langle 2, 2 \rangle, \langle 2, 1 \rangle\}$ and $\{\langle 2, 2 \rangle, \langle 2, 3 \rangle, \langle 3, 3 \rangle, \langle 3, 2 \rangle\}$, respectively.

« *Parenthetical remark.* Where $\mathcal{X}$ is any set, we sometimes write '$\mathcal{X}^n$' for the n-fold product of $\mathcal{X}$. For example, $\mathcal{X}^2$ is just $\mathcal{X} \times \mathcal{X}$, and $\mathcal{X}^3$ is $\mathcal{X}^2 \times \mathcal{X}$, that is, $\mathcal{X} \times \mathcal{X} \times \mathcal{X}$, and so on. *End remark.* »

3.3 Relations

For our purposes, we will think of relations as sets. We'll first focus on *binary relations*, and then briefly generalize to all n-ary relations.[8]

Definition 15. (Relations) *A* binary relation $\mathcal{R}$ *is just a set of ordered pairs.*

For convenience, we will sometimes (perhaps often) use '$x\mathcal{R}y$' to mean that $\langle x, y \rangle$ is in $\mathcal{R}$.

---

[8]Actually, as we'll see, there's a clear sense in which all relations, at least treated extensionally, just are binary relations, given our approach to ordered n-tuples above.

It is useful to define the *domain* and *range* of relations. Where $\mathcal{R}$ is a binary relation, we define the domain of $\mathcal{R}$, namely $dom(\mathcal{R})$, and the range of $\mathcal{R}$, namely $ran(\mathcal{R})$, as follows.

Definition 16. (Domain) $dom(\mathcal{R}) = \{x : \langle x, y \rangle \in \mathcal{R} \text{ for some } y\}$.

Definition 17. (Range) $ran(\mathcal{R}) = \{y : \langle x, y \rangle \in \mathcal{R} \text{ for some } x\}$.

In other words, $dom(\mathcal{R})$ contains all of the things that $\mathcal{R}$ relates to something or other, while $ran(\mathcal{R})$ contains all the things *to which* $\mathcal{R}$ relates something or other.

Consider the example of *loves*, which is a binary relation that obtains between objects x and y just if x loves y. On our account, the relation *loves* is a set $\mathcal{R}$ that contains ordered pairs $\langle x, y \rangle$, in particular, $\mathcal{R}$ contains all and only those pairs $\langle x, y \rangle$ such that x loves y. The *domain* of $\mathcal{R}$, in this case, contains all of the *lovers* (i.e., anyone who loves something), while the *range* of $\mathcal{R}$ contains all of the *beloved* (i.e., anyone who is loved by someone or other). So, if Max loves Agnes, then $\langle$Max, Agnes$\rangle \in \mathcal{R}$, and Max is in $dom(\mathcal{R})$ while Agnes is in $ran(\mathcal{R})$.[9]

What about n-ary relations, in general? The answer is the same: they are sets of ordered n-tuples. So, for example, a ternary relation—e.g., x *is between* y *and* z—is a set of triples, and so on. Of course, given our general account of n-tuples (see above), we have it that, for any $n \geq 2$, an n-ary relation is just a set of ordered pairs, where the first coordinate is an $n - 1$-tuple.[10]

3.3.1 *A few features of binary relations*

Some (binary) relations have various notable properties. The properties in question are as follows (where we assume that all of the x, y, and z are in the given relation's domain or range, that is, in the 'field' of the relation).

Definition 18. (Reflexivity) *A binary relation R is* reflexive *iff xRx for all x. (In other words: R is reflexive iff everything stands in R to itself.)*

---

[9] Using the idea of 'union' above, we can also define the *field* of a relation $\mathcal{R}$ to be the union of $dom(\mathcal{R})$ and $ran(\mathcal{R})$, that is, $field(\mathcal{R}) = dom(\mathcal{R}) \cup ran(\mathcal{R})$.

[10] See the Kuratowski definition in §3.2 to see the point. For present purposes, you can just think of n-ary relations as sets of ordered n-tuples.

Definition 19. (Symmetry) *A binary relation R is* symmetric *iff if xRy then yRx, for all x and y.*

Definition 20. (Transitivity) *A binary relation R is* transitive *iff if xRy and yRz then xRz, for all x, y, and z.*

Definition 21. (Equivalence) *A binary relation R is an* equivalence relation *iff R is reflexive, symmetric, and transitive.*

We won't need to explicitly invoke these notions (e.g., reflexivity, etc.) until Chapters 8 and 11; however, they're useful to think about in general. (Can you come up with examples of a reflexive relation? What about a symmetric relation? What of an equivalence relation?)

3.4   Functions

The idea of a *function* will be particularly useful in subsequent chapters. The foregoing work pays off, since functions are now very easy to define; they are simply special kinds of relations.

Definition 22. (Functions) *An n-ary function is an n-ary relation $\mathcal{R}$ such that, for any $x \in dom(\mathcal{R})$, there's exactly one y such that $x\mathcal{R}y$.*

So, what makes a relation $\mathcal{R}$ a *function* is the special 'unique value' (or 'unique second coordinate') constraint, namely, that functions never relate an item to more than one item. While a relation, in general, can relate an object x to as many different objects as it pleases, a *function* can do no such thing. To be a *function*, a relation must satisfy the given *unique second coordinate* condition: it can never relate something to two different things. Put in 'picture' terms (well, sort of), if you see a relation that contains the following pairs

$$\langle a, b \rangle , \langle a, c \rangle$$

then you know that the relation is either not a function or else $b = c$.

Notation. Since functions are just relations, we could continue to use the notation we've used for relations; however, it is convenient to use more familiar notation in the case of functions. Accordingly, we'll use 'f', 'g' and the like for functions, and when

$\langle x, y \rangle \in f$, we'll write '$f(x) = y$'. When $f(x) = y$, we say that y is the *value* of f at *argument* x.[11] So, in particular, when $f(x) = y$, we say that $f(x)$ is the value of f at x (where, in this case, that value is y).

A function is said to be a *unary function* if it takes single objects as arguments (or 'inputs'), as opposed to *pairs* of objects. So, for example, the function f defined over natural numbers by

$$f(x) = x + 1$$

is a unary function that takes a single number and yields (as value) the given number's successor. In particular, the value of (our given) f at 0 is 1, that is, $f(0) = 1$. Moreover, $f(1) = 2$, and $f(2) = 3$, and so on.

An example of a so-called *binary* function, which takes a *pair* as 'input', is the addition function g over natural numbers, namely,

$$g(x, y) = x + y$$

Function g, so defined, takes *ordered pairs* of numbers and yields a (unique) number.[12]

Notice that unary and binary functions can be specified in table form. For example, we can specify a tiny fragment of the successor function f as follows, where, as above, the successor function takes any (natural) number x to $x + 1$.

f	
1	0
2	1
3	2
4	3

Here, the argument (the input) of f is displayed in the right column and its corresponding value (the output) on the left. (So,

---

[11]Yes, this is an unfortunate use of the term 'argument'! Alas, the terminology is fairly settled. Fortunately, context will always clarify whether we're talking about a *function's* arguments (i.e., its inputs) or an *argument* in the sense of premises and conclusion.

[12]Binary functions, then, are really ternary relations, that is, sets of ordered triples. So, g, so defined, contains ordered triples like $\langle \langle 0, 0 \rangle, 0 \rangle$, $\langle \langle 1, 0 \rangle, 1 \rangle$, and so on.

e.g., if input x is 0, then the output $f(0)$ is 1, which is displayed on the left in the first row under 'f' in the table able.) Similarly, we can specify a tiny fragment of the (binary) addition function g, as given above, in tabular form, where the arguments (the inputs) are taken pairwise from the leftmost column and first row (e.g., $\langle 0, 0 \rangle$, $\langle 0, 1 \rangle$, etc.) and the values from the intersecting cell.

g	0	1	2	3
0	0	1	2	3
1	1	2	3	4
2	2	3	4	5
3	3	4	5	6

Regardless of how they are described, be it in tabular or some other form, a relation counts as *function* if and only if it satisfies the given uniqueness condition: namely, you never have $h(x) \neq h(y)$ if $x = y$.

3.5   Sets as tools

For our purposes, the foregoing ideas will give us most of the tools that we need for subsequent chapters. Modern logic, as suggested in Chapter 2, uses so-called formal languages to model the consequence relation of some target natural language. Such formal languages are frequently defined set-theoretically. While we will not be overly rigorous in subsequent chapters, we will use our acquired set-theoretic tools to model various accounts of 'cases' and, in turn, *truth in a case* relations. (See previous chapter.)

Summary and looking ahead

Summary. Sets are (possibly empty) collections of things that satisfy some entry condition, with each set coming equipped with an entry condition. Something is in a given set if and only if it satisfies the given entry condition. Two sets are identical iff they have exactly the same members. Ordered sets are sets with an ordering constraint: two ordered sets are the same iff they have the same elements *in the same order*. Ordered pairs are ordered sets of two elements. (Ordered n-tuples are ordered pairs where the first element is an ordered set of $n - 1$ elements.) *Relations* are simply sets of ordered pairs. The domain of a relation $\mathcal{R}$ is whatever is $\mathcal{R}$-related to something else, and the range contains everything to which $\mathcal{R}$ relates something. Functions are a special sort of relation, namely, all of those relations that relate nothing to more than one (distinct) thing.

Looking Ahead. In the next few chapters, we will put such set-theoretic tools to use in thinking about different logical theories and the phenomena that motivate them.

Further Reading. Any book on so-called naïve set theory will be useful for further study. An accessible text for independent study of contemporary (axiomatic) set theory is Goldrei 1996, which in turn will point to even further reading.

Exercises

1. Write out $\mathcal{Y} \times \mathcal{Z}$ and $\mathcal{Z} \times \mathcal{Y}$, where $\mathcal{Y} = \{1,2\}$ and $\mathcal{Z} = \{a,b,c\}$. Are $\mathcal{Y} \times \mathcal{Z}$ and $\mathcal{Z} \times \mathcal{Y}$ the same set? Justify your answer.

2. Using definition by abstraction, give brace-notation names (i.e., names formed using '{' and '}' as per the chapter) for each of the following sets.
    (a) The set of all even numbers.
    (b) The set of all felines.
    (c) The set of all tulips.
    (d) The set of all possible worlds.
    (e) The set of all people who love cats.

3. Assume that a, b, c, and d are distinct (i.e., non-identical) things. Which of the following relations are functions? (Also, if you weren't given that the various things are distinct, could you tell whether any of the following are functions? If so, why? If not, why not?)
    (a) $\{\langle a,a \rangle, \langle b,b \rangle, \langle c,c \rangle, \langle d,d \rangle\}$
    (b) $\{\langle a,d \rangle, \langle b,d \rangle, \langle c,d \rangle, \langle d,d \rangle\}$
    (c) $\{\langle a,b \rangle, \langle a,c \rangle, \langle b,d \rangle, \langle d,d \rangle\}$
    (d) $\{\langle b,a \rangle, \langle c,d \rangle, \langle a,a \rangle, \langle b,d \rangle\}$
    (e) $\{\langle d,d \rangle, \langle d,b \rangle, \langle b,d \rangle, \langle a,d \rangle\}$

4. Consider the relation of *biological motherhood*, which holds between objects x and y if and only if y is the biological mother of x. Is this relation a function? Justify your answer.

5. Consider the relation of *loves*, which holds between objects x and y if and only if x loves y. Is this relation a function? Justify your answer.

6. Since functions are relations, and all relations have a domain and range, it follows that functions have a domain and range. We say that the *domain* of a function f is the set of f's arguments (or 'inputs'), and the *range* of f is the set of f's values (or 'outputs'). Let the domain of g be $\{1, 2, 3\}$, where g is defined as follows.

$$g(x) = x + 22$$

What is the range of g?

7. Let $\mathcal{X} = \{1, 2\}$ and $\mathcal{Y} = \{\text{Max, Agnes}\}$. Specify *all* (non-empty) functions whose domain is $\mathcal{X}$ and range is $\mathcal{Y}$.

8. Specify all (non-empty) subsets of $\{1, 2, 3\}$.

9. Show why each of the following are true for any sets $\mathcal{X}$ and $\mathcal{Y}$.
   (a) If $\mathcal{X} \neq \mathcal{Y}$, then $\mathcal{X} \cap \mathcal{Y} \subset \mathcal{X} \cup \mathcal{Y}$.
   (b) If $\mathcal{X} \subset \mathcal{Y}$, then $\mathcal{X} \cup \mathcal{Y} = \mathcal{Y}$.
   (c) If $\mathcal{X} \subset \mathcal{Y}$, then $\mathcal{X} \cap \mathcal{Y} \subset \mathcal{Y}$.

10. Let f be some function with $dom(f) = \mathcal{X}$ (i.e., the domain of f is $\mathcal{X}$), for some arbitrary (non-empty) set $\mathcal{X}$. We say that our function f is a function *from* $\mathcal{X}$ *into* $\mathcal{Y}$ if $ran(f) \subseteq \mathcal{Y}$. Given this terminology, specify *all* (non-empty) functions from $\{A, B\}$ *into* $\{1, 2, 3\}$, where A and B are distinct sentences. (Note that any such function must map *every* element of the domain to something in $\{1, 2, 3\}$.)

11. Let $\mathcal{X}$ be an arbitrary set and f an arbitrary function. We say that f is an *operator on* $\mathcal{X}$ if and only if the $dom(f) = \mathcal{X}$ and $ran(f) \subseteq \mathcal{X}$. Consider the following operator on $\{1, 0\}$.

$$g(x) = 1 - x$$

Now, imagine a function v that assigns either 1 or 0 to each atomic sentence of our language, so that, for any atomic sentence A of our language, we have it that $v(A) = 1$ or $v(A) = 0$. Answer the following questions.
   (a) Suppose that $v(A) = 1$. What is $g(v(A))$?

(b) Suppose that $v(A) = 0$. What is $g(v(A))$?

(c) If $v(A) = 1$, what is $g(g(v(A)))$?

(d) Is it true that $g(g(x)) = 1$ just when $x = 1$?

(e) How, *if at all*, is the given function g similar to negation (as you thought about it in Chapter 2)?

Sample answers

Here are some sample answers. (In the first one, the answer is somewhat involved for purposes of illustrating, in a fairly step-by-step fashion, how one might go about proving the given claims.)

Answer 9b. We have to show that if $\mathcal{X} \subset \mathcal{Y}$, then $\mathcal{X} \cup \mathcal{Y} = \mathcal{Y}$. We show this (viz., the given conditional) by so-called conditional proof: we assume that the antecedent is true (viz., that $\mathcal{X} \subset \mathcal{Y}$), and then show—via valid steps (!)—that the consequent is true. (Usually, we do this simply by invoking definitions involved.) So, suppose that $\mathcal{X} \subset \mathcal{Y}$, in which case, by definition of *proper subset* (see Def. 11), it follows that anything in $\mathcal{X}$ is in $\mathcal{Y}$, and that $\mathcal{Y}$ contains something that $\mathcal{X}$ doesn't contain. Now, we need to show the consequent of our target conditional: viz., that $\mathcal{X} \cup \mathcal{Y} = \mathcal{Y}$. This is an identity claim: it claims that the two given sets are identical. How do we show that they're identical? Well, we have to invoke the definition of identity for sets, which tells us that, in this case, $\mathcal{X} \cup \mathcal{Y} = \mathcal{Y}$ iff both $\mathcal{X} \cup \mathcal{Y}$ and $\mathcal{Y}$ contain exactly the same things. In other words, we show that $\mathcal{X} \cup \mathcal{Y} = \mathcal{Y}$ by showing that something (no matter what it is) is in $\mathcal{X} \cup \mathcal{Y}$ if and only if it's in $\mathcal{Y}$. So, in effect, we have to show that two different conditionals are true to show that the two sets are identical:

9b.1 If something (no matter what it is) is in $\mathcal{X} \cup \mathcal{Y}$, it is in $\mathcal{Y}$.

9b.2 If something (no matter what it is) is in $\mathcal{Y}$, it is in $\mathcal{X} \cup \mathcal{Y}$.

And here, we can just do so-called conditional proofs again for each of (9b.1) and (9b.2): we assume the given antecedents and show, via valid steps (usually just appealing to the definitions), that the given consequents follow. So, for (9b.1), we assume that something—call it (no matter what it is) 'z'—is in $\mathcal{X} \cup \mathcal{Y}$. What we have to show is that z is in $\mathcal{Y}$. Well, by assumption, we have that $z \in \mathcal{X} \cup \mathcal{Y}$, in which case, *by definition of union* (see Def. 8), if $z \in \mathcal{X} \cup \mathcal{Y}$ then $z \in \mathcal{X}$ *or* $z \in \mathcal{Y}$. In the latter case, we have what we want (viz., that $z \in \mathcal{Y}$). What about the former case in which $z \in \mathcal{X}$? Do we also get that $z \in \mathcal{Y}$? Yes: we get this from our initial supposition that $\mathcal{X} \subset \mathcal{Y}$, which assures that anything in $\mathcal{X}$ is in $\mathcal{Y}$. What this tells us is that, either way, if something z (no matter what z may be) is in $\mathcal{X} \cup \mathcal{Y}$, then it's also in $\mathcal{Y}$ (provided that, as we've assumed from the start, $\mathcal{X} \subset \mathcal{Y}$). And this is what we wanted to show for (9b.1).

With respect to (9b.2), we assume that something z (no matter what z is) is in $\mathcal{Y}$. We need to show that $z \in \mathcal{X} \cup \mathcal{Y}$. But this follows immediately from the definition of union (see Def. 8).[13] According to the definition, something is in $\mathcal{X} \cup \mathcal{Y}$ if and only if it's either in $\mathcal{X}$ or in $\mathcal{Y}$. Hence, given that (by supposition) $z \in \mathcal{Y}$, we have it that $z \in \mathcal{X} \cup \mathcal{Y}$.

Taking stock of Answer 9.b. What we've proved, in showing (9b.1) and (9b.2), is that, under our assumption that $\mathcal{X} \subset \mathcal{Y}$, something (no matter what it is) is in $\mathcal{X} \cup \mathcal{Y}$ iff it's in $\mathcal{Y}$. By definition of identity for sets (see Def. 7), this tells us that, under our assumption that $\mathcal{X} \subset \mathcal{Y}$, the sets $\mathcal{X} \cup \mathcal{Y}$ and $\mathcal{Y}$ are identical. And this is what (9b) required us to show.

Answer 11a. If $v(A)$ is 1, then, plugging 1 in for x in the definition of function g, we have that $g(1) = 1 - 1$, and so $g(v(A))$ is 0.

---

[13]Well, we're assuming that so-called Addition is valid, that is, that a disjunction is implied by either of its disjuncts. Some logical theories question this (see, e.g., Chapter 12 in which one such theory is briefly waved at); however, we'll assume it in our reasoning throughout the book.

PART II

BASIC CONNECTIVES

4

Classical Theory

I dreamt that life was wholly precise: black/white, on/off...
                                            – Anonymous

In this chapter we introduce the so-called classical approach to some basic connectives, and, in turn, introduce the corresponding classical theory of logical consequence.[1] The basic connectives in question are conjunction, disjunction, and negation. These connectives, in addition to a few defined ones (see §4.6), will occupy our attention in this chapter and the next two chapters.[2]

A chief aim of logical theories is to specify the logical behavior of connectives—in this case, the behavior of our basic connectives, conjunction, disjunction, and negation. Specifying the logical behavior of connectives involves giving an account of logical consequence—of validity—for the language (or fragment thereof) that contains those connectives. Doing *that*, as suggested in Chapters 1 and 2, involves specifying one's 'cases' and giving an account of *truth in a case* for the various connectives—in short, giving 'truth conditions' for the various connectives. In this chapter, we'll look at the basic *classical* approach to these issues, at least for the given connectives.

4.1 Cases: complete and consistent

Recall, from Chapter 1, the two chief ingredients involved in our 'recipe' for logical consequence: *cases* and *truth in a case*. The latter ingredient concerns truth conditions for connectives, something to which we explicitly turn below. For now, let us introduce

---

[1]The term 'classical' in this context is entrenched (and also applies to richer languages discussed in later chapters). It is controversial as to whether the target (so-called) classical logical theory is the logical theory endorsed by classical thinkers (e.g., Aristotle). It is perhaps best to think of the term 'classical' along the lines of 'standard' or 'common'.

[2]We will consider more connectives in subsequent chapters.

some terminology to talk about different 'kinds' of cases—leaving aside the question of what, exactly, the 'nature' of such cases might be.

In the following definitions, $\mathcal{L}$ is a given language with at least the basic connectives conjunction, disjunction, and negation.[3] As in Chapter 2, we let $\neg$ be negation, $\wedge$ conjunction, and $\vee$ disjunction.

Definition 23. (Complete Cases) *A case c is* complete *if and only if either A is true-in-c or $\neg A$ is true-in-c, for any A in $\mathcal{L}$.*

Definition 24. (Consistent Cases) *A case c is* consistent *if and only if there is no A in $\mathcal{L}$ such that both A and $\neg A$ are true-in c.*

We shall use this terminology to classify different sorts of cases (and corresponding logical theories). In particular, a distinguishing feature of the classical logical theory is that it takes all cases to be both complete and consistent (in the given sense): nothing is a classical case unless it is complete and consistent. While this does not fully define classical cases, it marks out a key feature that distinguishes them from other sorts of cases discussed in subsequent chapters. Before giving a fuller account of classical cases, we turn to the matter of 'truth conditions' (strictly, truth-in-a-case conditions) for the basic connectives.

« *Parenthetical remark.* As will be evident throughout, the tasks of specifying *cases* and specifying *truth in a case*—the two chief tasks in our approach to specifying theories of consequence—are intimately related (especially when *cases* are treated only abstractly as things in which claims are true). We will, in fact, be mostly focusing on logical theories that take cases to be (in effect) the same with respect to the logical behavior of disjunctions and conjunctions (and related logical machinery introduced later). As such, we sometimes speak of completeness and consistency (see definitions above) as being definitive of classical cases, even though this is not strictly correct. (As will be clear below, classical cases also have features concerning, e.g., disjunctions and conjunctions.) *End parenthetical.* »

---

[3]This chapter assumes that the given three connectives are our only (basic) connectives.

4.2 Classical 'truth conditions'

For our purposes, truth conditions are *truth-in-a-case* conditions. Each connective determines a type of (molecular) sentence, namely, a molecular sentence whose principal connective is the given connective.[4] For example, consider negation. Suppose that you have some sentence A. To form a *negation* (one type of molecular sentence), you simply apply negation, which becomes the principal connective (of the resulting negation). Given your initial A, you apply negation to get $\neg A$, which is the negation of A. Similarly, suppose that you have two sentences A and B, and you apply conjunction; you thereby form a conjunction (another type of molecular sentence), namely, $A \wedge B$, which is the conjunction of A and B. The same idea applies to the other connective(s).

With three connectives, then, we have three different types of molecular sentence: conjunctions, disjunctions, and negations. In giving truth-in-a-case conditions (what we're calling 'truth conditions'), one specifies what it takes for each type of sentence to be true-in-a-case.

Before turning to the truth conditions for connectives (i.e., for our different molecular sentences), it's important to recall that, in addition to our molecular sentences, we also have our *atomic* sentences—sentences with no connectives. What about truth-in-a-case conditions for such atomics? For present purposes, we will skip (for now) what it takes for an atomic sentence to be true-in-a-case, and we'll just assume—in accord with constraints on classical cases—that every atomic is either true-in-a-case or it's not, in which case its negation is true-in-the-given-case (since these are classical, and so complete, cases).

To be slightly clearer, let us use '$c \models_1 A$' to abbreviate that A is true-in-c, and similarly use '$c \not\models_1 A$' to abbreviate that A is *not* true-in-c. That classical cases are complete and consistent amounts to the claim that, for any sentence A and any (classical) case c, we have it that either $c \models_1 A$ or $c \models_1 \neg A$ but not both. In particular, then, we have it that, for any *atomic* A and any

---

[4]If we were being fully rigorous, we would precisely define what it is to be a 'principal connective'. This is something that is covered in standard introductions to formal logic. We will content ourselves with a loose but, hopefully, adequate account.

(classical) case c, either $c \models_1 A$ or $c \models_1 \neg A$. This leaves open the question of *how* atomics 'get to be true' in such cases, but we can set this question aside for now.[5] For present purposes, we don't really need to know *how* atomics come to be true-in-a-case; we just need to know that, for any classical case c, every atomic is either true-in-c or its negation is true-in-c, in which case the atomic is *not* true-in-c.

With the assumption regarding atomics in hand, we can now specify the classical truth conditions for *all* sentences (or 'sentence types') in our given language.

Definition 25. (Basic Classical Truth Conditions) *Where c is any case, and A and B any sentences of $\mathcal{L}$, the classical conditions for the basic connectives are as follows.*

> *Conjunction: $c \models_1 A \wedge B$ iff $c \models_1 A$ and $c \models_1 B$.*
>
> *Disjunction: $c \models_1 A \vee B$ iff $c \models_1 A$ or $c \models_1 B$ (or both).*[6]
>
> *Negation: $c \models_1 \neg A$ iff $c \not\models_1 A$.*

This tells us that, according to the classical theory, a conjunction is true-in-a-case just if both conjuncts are true-in-that-case. Similarly, a disjunction is true-in-a-case iff at least one of the disjuncts is true-in-the-case. Finally, we have it that a negation is true-in-a-case just if the negatum is not true-in-the-given-case.

We shall say that a *classical case*—or, at least, a *basic* classical case (i.e., a 'classical case' as far as the basic connectives go)—is any complete and consistent case that 'obeys' the basic classical truth conditions.

For convenience, let us define a standard notion of *falsity* as 'truth of negation'. More precisely, let us say that A is *false-in-a-case* if and only if $\neg A$ is true-in-the-given-case. Something that you should think about is that, on the classical account, A is false-in-c if and only if $c \not\models_1 A$. After all, given the above truth conditions for negation, we have it that $c \models_1 \neg A$ if and only if $c \not\models_1 A$. By our definition, A is *false-in-c* if and only if $c \models_1 \neg A$.

---

[5] The question is taken up in later chapters.

[6] This parenthetical 'or both' is important; it marks the *inclusive* usage of 'or'. This inclusive usage is what, unless otherwise stated, we use throughout the book, and so such parenthetical notes 'or both' are often omitted.

Putting these together (plus the constraints on classical cases above), we see that A is false-in-c if and only if $c \not\models_1 A$.

« *Parenthetical remark.* Looking ahead, we can present things more broadly by introducing not only a *truth in case c* relation $\models_1$, but also a *falsity in c* relation $\models_0$. In the classical framework, $\models_0$ simply winds up being definable as $\not\models_1$ (i.e., the *falsity in a case* relation winds up being the so-called complement of the *truth in a case* relation—that is, the *not* true-in-a-case relation. As such, the separate *falsity in a case* relation is superfluous in the classical setting, but it will be important in later chapters. *End parenthetical.* »

4.3 Basic classical consequence

With the foregoing truth conditions and account of *cases*, we now have an idea of the classical theory of logical consequence (at least for the basic connectives). Consider, for example, the following argument form.

$$\neg\neg A \therefore A$$

Is this valid according to the classical theory? The answer is *yes*. After all, an argument is valid if and only if there's no counterexample. Can there be a counterexample to $\neg\neg A \therefore A$? What we're asking is whether there can be a (classical) case in which $\neg\neg A$ is true but A false. In other words, we want to know whether there's a (classical) case c such that $c \models_1 \neg\neg A$ but $c \not\models_1 A$.[7]

To answer the current question, we have to rely on the classical account of 'cases' and, in particular, the given truth conditions for negation. To see that $\neg\neg A \therefore A$ is classically valid (i.e., valid according to the classical account of consequence), we can reason as follows. Let c be an arbitrary classical case in which $\neg\neg A$ is true, i.e., a classical case c such that $c \models_1 \neg\neg A$. According to the truth condition for negation, we have it that

$$c \models \neg\neg A \text{ if and only if } c \not\models \neg A$$

---

[7]Using the observation concerning falsity, the question may also be put thus: is there a (classical) case c such that $c \models_1 \neg\neg A$ but $c \models_1 \neg A$? (Why is this an equivalent, and perhaps more telling, way of asking the going question?)

that is, that $\neg\neg A$ is true-in-c if and only if $\neg A$ is not true-in-c. Since, by supposition, $c \models_1 \neg\neg A$, we have it that $c \not\models_1 \neg A$. But, now, recall that c is a classical case, c is *complete*, in which case, if $c \not\models_1 \neg A$ (i.e., if $\neg A$ is not true-in-c), then $c \models_1 A$ (i.e., A is true-in-c). Hence, any (classical) case in which $\neg\neg A$ is true is a case in which A is true. Equivalently, there's no (classical) case c such that $c \models_1 \neg\neg A$ but $c \not\models_1 A$, which means that there's no counterexample to the given argument form. Hence, by definition, the given argument form is valid. Consider another argument form, namely, $A \wedge B \therefore A$. Once again, we can see that this is classically valid by invoking our knowledge of classical cases and, in particular, the classical truth condition for conjunction. Can there be a (classical) case in which $A \wedge B$ is true but A not? Equivalently, can we have a (classical) case c such that $c \models_1 A \wedge B$ but $c \not\models_1 A$? No. The classical truth condition for conjunction tells us that, for any (classical) case c, if $c \models_1 A \wedge B$ then $c \models_1 A$ and $c \models_1 B$, in which case $c \models_1 A$. So, there's no counterexample, and hence the argument is valid.

With respect to disjunction, consider the argument form $A \therefore A \vee B$. Is this valid according to the classical theory? Yes. After all, the relevant truth condition tells us that if at least one disjunct is true-in-a-given-case, then the entire disjunction is true-in-the-given-case. In other words, we have it that if either $c \models_1 A$ or $c \models_1 B$ (or both), then $c \models_1 A \vee B$. Hence, in particular, if $c \models_1 A$ then $c \models_1 A \vee B$. So, there cannot be a case in which A is true but $A \vee B$ not true, and so cannot be a counterexample.

Also notable is that $A \vee \neg A$ is logically true, that is, true-in-*all (classical) cases*, that is, $c \models_1 A \vee \neg A$ for all (classical) c. In effect, the logical truth of $A \vee \neg A$ falls out of the *completeness* feature of classical cases and the truth conditions for disjunction. The truth conditions for disjunction tell us that a disjunction is true-in-a-case iff at least one of the disjuncts is true-in-the-given-case. Hence, the disjunction $A \vee \neg A$ is such that $c \models_1 A \vee \neg A$ iff $c \models_1 A$ or $c \models_1 \neg A$. Any classical case c is complete, which, in our terminology, means that either $c \models_1 A$ or $c \models_1 \neg A$ (but not both, by consistency). So, there cannot be a (classical) case in which $A \vee \neg A$ fails to be true. Hence, as above, $A \vee \neg A$ is logically true, according to the classical theory.

4.4   Motivation: precision

Before moving to a standard, formal picture of the basic classical account, one might wonder about the motivation behind the classical theory. Why, for example, think that our cases are complete and consistent? There are many answers that one might give to this question, but the basic idea is that our language—or the relevant fragment of it—is precise, in some sense.

The language of mathematics is often taken to be an example of a precise language. In mathematics,[8] we assume that every (mathematical) sentence is either true or false—that is, that either A or $\neg A$ is true, for every (mathematical) sentence A. Moreover, in mathematics, we assume that no sentence can be both true and false—that is, that not both A and $\neg A$ can be true. If one focuses chiefly on mathematics, or even takes mathematics to be the 'ideal example' of deductive validity, then the classical theory is well-motivated. Indeed, what is today called 'classical logic' (which includes the basic connectives above but also a bit more) was formulated as an account of logical consequence in (classical) mathematics.

Of course, one might—and many have—thought that the classical theory is the *right* theory for our language, in general (at least for the basic connectives). One might think, for example, that—even apart from mathematics—the very meaning of negation (in English, say) enjoys the classical truth conditions, and similarly enjoys the logical behaviour captured in the classical account. One might think the same thing about disjunction and conjunction, namely, that the classical truth conditions get things right. In particular, one might think that $A \vee \neg A$ is 'necessarily true', in some sense, and is as much in virtue of the very meaning of negation and disjunction. In short, one might think—and, again, many have thought—that the classical account gets more than our mathematical language right; it gets our language, in general, right (at least for the given basic connectives).

---

[8]Strictly speaking, what follows focuses on so-called *classical* mathematics, which is what most people think of when they think of mathematics. So-called *constructive* mathematics takes a different approach, one that we will ignore (only for simplicity).

On this way of thinking, we have it that every sentence, not only mathematical ones, are either true or false (but not both). Of course, given our finite circumstances, we might not be able to *know* the truth or falsity of every sentence, but this is a limitation on our part, not a blemish against the classical theory of logic. According to the classical theory, there's no 'indeterminacy' in the language at all, in the sense that, as above, every meaningful sentence is either true or false.

In subsequent chapters, we will (lightly) explore a few phenomena that challenge the classical approach to our basic connectives, at least when one applies that account beyond the language of mathematics. For now, we turn to a slightly more precise account of the classical theory; we turn to a 'formal picture' of the idea.

4.5   Formal picture

As throughout, the main aim of a logical theory is to specify the consequence relation of a given language. For our purposes, we are concentrating on a language with only a few basic connectives, and we are ignoring any structure within our atomic sentences. Our aim in this section is to briefly sketch a formal picture of the classical logical theory of such a language. Towards that end, we will give a sketch of a formal language, a sketch of the 'semantics' (viz., 'truth conditions') for the language, and then define the consequence relation on the given language. What follows presupposes the set-theoretic tools from Chapter 3.

4.5.1   *Syntax of $\mathcal{L}$*

Recall that, for our purposes, the *syntax* of a language specifies the basic (syntactic) ingredients of a language and defines what counts as a (grammatical) sentence in the language. We will define a simple syntax for the language $\mathcal{L}$.

Definition 26. (Syntax of $\mathcal{L}$) *The syntax of a language $\mathcal{L}$ contains ingredients and sentences.*

1. *Ingredients of $\mathcal{L}$*
    (a) *A set $\mathcal{A}$ of atomic sentences. This set contains the lowercase letters 'p', 'q', and 'r' with or without numerical subscripts.*

(b) *A set C of basic connectives. This set contains '¬', which is a unary connective, and also the binary connectives '∧' and '∨'.*

(c) *A set P of punctuation marks. This set contains '(' and ')'.*

2. *The set S of $\mathcal{L}$'s sentences is defined as follows.*

   (a) *Everything in $\mathcal{A}$ is in S.*

   (b) *If A and B are in S, then so too are $\neg A, (A \wedge B)$, and $(A \vee B)$.*

   (c) *Nothing else is in S (except what follows from the above two clauses).*

Clauses (1a)–(1c) of the definition specify the basic ingredients of $\mathcal{L}$, and in particular our basic connectives. Clauses (2a)–(2c) specify the set of sentences of $\mathcal{L}$. For example, we know that p is a sentence of $\mathcal{L}$. How do we know that? Well, we know, from (1a) that p is in $\mathcal{A}$, that is, that p is an atomic sentence of $\mathcal{L}$. In turn, (2a) tells us that everything in $\mathcal{A}$ (i.e., all atomics) is in S, that is, that everything in $\mathcal{A}$ is a sentence of $\mathcal{L}$.

Likewise, we know that $(p \vee q_{22})$ is a sentence of $\mathcal{L}$. After all, (1a) tells us that p and q_{22} are in $\mathcal{A}$, and so, by (2a), we know that p and q_{22} are in S (i.e., sentences of $\mathcal{L}$). Finally, (2b) tells us that the result of putting '∨' between two sentences, and enclosing the result with our punctuation marks, gives us a sentence of $\mathcal{L}$. So, since, as above, p and q_{22} are sentences, then so too is $(p \vee q_{22})$.

On the other hand, we can see that, for example, '¬ ∧ p' is not a sentence of $\mathcal{L}$. After all, clause (2c) tells us that nothing is a sentence of $\mathcal{L}$ unless it counts as such via clauses (2a) or (2b) or both. But there's no way to get '¬ ∧ p' from (2a) or (2b), and so it isn't a sentence. (Question: is $\neg(p)$ a sentence of $\mathcal{L}$?)

The foregoing, while quick, is enough syntax for our purposes. The pressing concern is the semantics—the 'truth conditions' for our sentences.

4.5.2 *Semantics of $\mathcal{L}$*

The chief aim of logic, as above, is to specify logical consequence for a given language. We are concentrating on the language $\mathcal{L}$, as above. To specify logical consequence, we have to say what our *cases* are and, in turn, give truth-in-a-case conditions for all sentences.

Since our concern, in this chapter, is with the basic classical theory, we need to think about how to 'model' our classical cases. We need our cases to be complete and consistent, in the sense above. One way of doing this is to take our cases to be special sets of sentences, and define *truth in a case* as nothing more than *being a member of a case*. This approach is natural and sufficient for our basic connectives, but we will resort to a slightly different approach that makes it easier to assess the classical theory. (See exercises.)

We begin with a set of 'semantic values',[9] in particular $\mathcal{V} = \{1, 0\}$. Intuitively, we can think of 1 as representing the semantic status 'truth', and 0 as representing 'falsity'. Our *cases*, in turn, will be functions from $\mathcal{S}$ (sentences) into $\mathcal{V}$. Let v be any such function. Since v is a function from $\mathcal{S}$ into $\mathcal{V}$, we have it that $v(A) = 1$ or $v(A) = 0$ for any sentence A. Hence, every atomic sentence of $\mathcal{L}$ gets assigned either 1 or 0 by any such function.

Let us define *truth in a case* as follows: A is true-in-a-case v (remember that our 'cases' are now functions) if and only if $v(A) = 1$. Similarly, A is *false-in-a-case* v if and only if $v(A) = 0$.

Notice that we do *not* want to allow just *any* old function from $\mathcal{S}$ into $\mathcal{V}$ to count as a classical case! After all, there are certainly functions from $\mathcal{S}$ into $\mathcal{V}$ that do not respect the classical truth conditions. Consider, for example, a function v such that $v(A \lor \neg A) = 0$. The classical theory, of course, has it that $A \lor \neg A$ is true-in-*every case*, and so our given function fouls up the classical theory if we allow it among our cases.

To rule out such 'unwanted' functions from our set of cases, we invoke the following truth conditions. In particular, we say that a function v, from $\mathcal{S}$ into $\mathcal{V}$, is a *classical case* if and only if it 'obeys' the following clauses—the following truth conditions—for all sentences A in B. (Here, 'or' is inclusive!)

- Conjunction: $v(A \land B) = 1$ iff $v(A) = 1 = v(B)$.
- Disjunction: $v(A \lor B) = 1$ iff $v(A) = 1$ or $v(B) = 1$.
- Negation: $v(\neg A) = 1$ iff $v(A) = 0$.

---

[9]These values are sometimes called 'truth values', but we'll use the broader term.

Equivalently, we can give such conditions via the following tables—sometimes called 'truth tables'. (For purposes of 'input' and 'output' values, these tables may be read along the lines of the unary- and binary-function tables displayed in §3.4.)

¬		∧	1	0	∨	1	0
0	1	1	1	0	1	1	1
1	0	0	0	0	0	1	0

Either way, we have succeeded in specifying both the truth-in-a-case conditions and, in turn, the 'right' set of cases—namely, the ones that 'obey' the given truth conditions.

The final step, in giving the semantics, is to specify our target relation: namely, logical consequence. The definition is just an instance of our recipe in Chapter 1.

Definition 27. (Basic Classical Consequence) *B is a logical consequence of A if and only if there is no classical case v such that $v(A) = 1$ but $v(B) = 0$.*

To make this more general, let us say that v *satisfies* a sentence A iff $v(A) = 1$ (i.e., iff A is true-in-the-given-case). In turn, let $\mathcal{X}$ be any set of $\mathcal{L}$ sentences. We say that v *satisfies* $\mathcal{X}$ iff v satisfies every member of $\mathcal{X}$. With this terminology, we can give a more general definition of basic classical consequence (instead of, as above, single-premise arguments).

Definition 28. (General Basic Classical Consequence) *A is a logical consequence of $\mathcal{X}$ if and only if there is no classical case v that satisfies $\mathcal{X}$ but not A.*

You should think about this definition, compare it with the 'general recipe' of logical consequence, and also evaluate various argument forms for (basic classical) validity.

By way of terminology, we will write '$\mathcal{X} \vdash A$' to mean that A is logical consequence of $\mathcal{X}$. One may also read '$\mathcal{X} \vdash A$' as saying that $\mathcal{X}$ *implies* A, which is shorthand for 'A is a logical consequence of $\mathcal{X}$'.[10] For example, we have seen that, according

---

[10]More accurately but somewhat more cumbersome: in saying that $\mathcal{X}$ implies A, where $\mathcal{X}$ is a set of sentences (versus a sentence), we really mean that the members of $\mathcal{X}$, taken together, imply A. For simplicity, we shall often slide over this distinction.

to the classical theory, $\neg\neg A \vdash A$, that is, that $\neg\neg A$ implies A. Similarly, we have seen that $A \vdash A \vee B$, that is, that $A \vee B$ is a consequence of A, that A implies $A \vee B$.

« *Long parenthetical remark.* In this book, we'll be looking at a handful of different logical theories, each pointing to a different consequence relation. At the moment, we have our basic classical consequence relation, which we might explicitly write as '$\vdash_{bc}$' (for *basic classical*). Other consequence relations may be denoted via different subscripts: $\vdash_x$, $\vdash_y$, or whathaveyou. While such subscripts will be important when more than one consequence relation (more than one logical theory) is under discussion, the subscripts can usually be dropped—and will be dropped. Throughout this book, we shall simply use the turnstile to mark the consequence relation under discussion: '$\mathcal{X} \vdash A$' may be read as saying that $\mathcal{X}$ implies A *according to the logical theory under discussion.* (So, e.g., in the current chapter, '$\mathcal{X} \vdash A$' says that $\mathcal{X}$ implies A *according to the basic classical theory*, where the basic classical consequence relation is defined as above. In the next chapter, where we look at a so-called paracomplete theory, '$\mathcal{X} \vdash A$' says that $\mathcal{X}$ implies A *according to the basic paracomplete theory*, where this theory—and its target consequence relation—are defined in the next chapter. And so on.) Again, when more than one consequence relation is being discussed (e.g., for comparative purposes), a subscript shall be introduced. *End long parenthetical.* »

4.6   Defined connectives

Before examining the classical theory a little bit further, it is important to note that, in addition to our basic three connectives (above), we can also recognize some so-called derivative or defined connectives, in particular, some *conditional*-like connectives.

For example, suppose that we write '$A \rightarrow B$' as *shorthand* for $\neg A \vee B$. In many ways, '$A \rightarrow B$' behaves like a conditional, that is, like (some uses of) an 'If ... then ...' sentence. Treating $\rightarrow$ as a conditional, we call A the *antecedent* of $A \rightarrow B$, and we call B the *consequent*.

Since $\rightarrow$ is a defined connective—that is, it's defined in terms of ones we already have—we don't need to give further truth conditions for it. The truth conditions for $A \rightarrow B$ are simply the truth conditions for $\neg A \vee B$, which can be figured out by looking at our basic truth-in-a-case conditions above. In particular:

$$v(A \rightarrow B) = 1 \text{ iff either } v(A) = 0 \text{ or } v(B) = 1 \text{ (or both).}$$

So, our conditional—which, when defined in terms of negation and disjunction, is called a *material conditional*—is true-in-a-case iff it has a false antecedent or a true consequent in the given case.

Similarly, we can introduce another defined connective, namely, a biconditional. We will let '$A \leftrightarrow B$' abbreviate $(A \rightarrow B) \wedge (B \rightarrow A)$. (Notice that we're already utilizing our first defined connective, our material conditional.) Like the conditional, we need not introduce new truth conditions for $\leftrightarrow$, since its truth-in-a-case conditions are already given by the conditions for conjunction and the conditional (whose truth conditions, as above, are given in terms of disjunction and negation). In particular, the truth-in-a-case conditions for $A \leftrightarrow B$ are simply those for $(A \rightarrow B) \wedge (B \rightarrow A)$, which are

$$v(A \leftrightarrow B) = 1 \text{ iff } v(A) = v(B)$$

So, a biconditional is true-in-a-case exactly if the two component sentences have the same semantic value in that case; otherwise, the biconditional is false-in-the-given-case.

The truth conditions for $\rightarrow$ and $\leftrightarrow$ may be equivalently given via the following tables.

$\rightarrow$	1	0		$\leftrightarrow$	1	0
1	1	0		1	1	0
0	1	1		0	0	1

4.7 Some notable valid forms

Any logical theory of a language provides an account of the (logical) behavior of the language's connectives. In part, a theory of the connectives is largely reflected in the theory's given truth conditions for the connectives, and the associated account of 'cases'. Still, where the behavior is manifest is in the consequence relation, in particular, the valid argument forms involving those connectives. Some representative forms that, on the classical theory, are valid are as follows.[11]

- Excluded Middle (LEM): $\vdash A \vee \neg A$
- Non-Contradiction: $\vdash \neg(A \wedge \neg A)$
- Modus Ponens: $A \rightarrow B, A \vdash B$
- Modus Tollens: $A \rightarrow B, \neg B \vdash \neg A$
- Disjunctive Syllogism: $A \vee B, \neg A \vdash B$
- Contraposition: $A \rightarrow B \dashv\vdash \neg B \rightarrow \neg A$
- Explosion (EFQ):[12] $A, \neg A \vdash B$
- Addition: $A \vdash A \vee B$
- Adjunction: $A, B \vdash A \wedge B$
- Simplification: $A \wedge B \vdash A$
- De Morgan: $\neg(A \vee B) \dashv\vdash \neg A \wedge \neg B$
- De Morgan: $\neg(A \wedge B) \dashv\vdash \neg A \vee \neg B$
- Double Negation: $\neg\neg A \dashv\vdash A$

There are other notable forms that are valid according to the classical theory, but the foregoing give a representative flavor.

In establishing that an argument form is valid according to a given theory, one must invoke the theory's account of consequence, and in particular its account of *cases* and *truth in a case*. By way of example, we will close with establishing the validity of Disjunctive Syllogism and Contraposition, respectively.

To see that $A \vee B, \neg A \vdash B$, that is, that Disjunctive Syllogism is valid, we can reason as follows. The given argument form is valid iff there is no classical case in which the premises are true and the conclusion false. Our classical cases are functions that obey the given truth conditions (see above). Let v be such a function, and suppose that the given premises are all true in (or according to) v, that is, that $v(A \vee B) = 1 = v(\neg A)$. Since $v(\neg A) = 1$, the truth conditions for negation tell us that $v(A) = 0$. But, now, the

---

[11]Notation: we let '$\vdash A$' (without anything to the left of the turnstile) mean that A is logically true according to the given theory. Also, we write '$A \dashv\vdash B$' to mean that A implies B and B implies A (according to the given theory). Finally, for readability's sake, outermost parentheses are dropped, which are otherwise strictly required by the syntax of $\mathcal{L}$.

[12]This is sometimes called *Ex Falso Quodlibet*.

truth conditions for disjunction tell us that $v(A \vee B) = 1$ iff either $v(A) = 1$ or $v(B) = 1$. By supposition, $v(A \vee B) = 1$, and so, since we have it that $v(A) = 0$, it must be that $v(B) = 1$. Given that v was an arbitrary case, we conclude that there cannot be any classical case in which both $A \vee B$ and $\neg A$ are true but B is false. Hence, there's no counterexample to the given argument form. Hence, Disjunctive Syllogism is classically valid.

For the other example, namely, Contraposition, we want to show that there's no case in which $A \rightarrow B$ is true but $\neg B \rightarrow \neg A$ is false. Again, we simply use our given truth conditions. Let v be an arbitrary classical case. According to the truth condition for $A \rightarrow B$, we have it that if $v(A \rightarrow B) = 1$, then either $v(A) = 0$ or $v(B) = 1$. If the former holds, then $v(\neg B \rightarrow \neg A) = 1$, given that its consequent is true (see the truth condition for negation). If the latter holds, $v(\neg B \rightarrow \neg A) = 1$, since its antecedent is false. Hence, either way, so long as $v(A \rightarrow B) = 1$, we have it that $v(\neg B \rightarrow \neg A) = 1$. Given that v was arbitrary, we conclude that there cannot be a classical case in which $A \rightarrow B$ is true but $\neg B \rightarrow \neg A$ not true. Hence, Contraposition is classically valid.

4.8   Summary and looking ahead

Summary. Concentrating only on the basic language $\mathcal{L}$, the classical theory takes cases to be 'complete and consistent', where such cases are modeled by functions from sentences into the semantic value set $\{1, 0\}$. The truth conditions for $\mathcal{L}$'s connectives are fairly natural, namely, that a negation is true-in-c iff its negand (or negatum) is false-in-c; a conjunction is true-in-c iff both conjuncts are true-in-c; and a disjunction is true-in-c iff at least one disjunct is true-in-c. Logical consequence is defined as per the recipe of Chapter 1, with the ingredients of *cases* and *truth in a case* filled out classically as above. In addition to our basic connectives—namely, negation, conjunction, disjunction—we also have defined connectives, a (material) conditional and biconditional. The truth conditions for these defined connectives are already given via the connectives (and *their* truth conditions) in terms of which the defined connectives are defined.

Philosophically, the classical theory has it that our language is entirely 'precise'. Every sentence is true or false: there's no 'indeterminacy'. Moreover, there's no 'over-determinacy', in the sense that no sentence is both true and false.

Looking Ahead. In the next chapter, we will briefly explore a rival logical theory, a theory that agrees with the classical theory about the set of basic logical connectives, but disagrees about the truth conditions and, in particular, the 'cases'. The next chapter briefly examines a theory that rejects the idea that our language is fully precise, instead accepting that, in some sense, our language allows for 'indeterminacy'.

Further Reading. Almost any of the many, many, many introductory logic textbooks will provide useful, supplemental discussion of the classical theory of our basic connectives. Three slightly more advanced books that are closely related to the presentation here but go into much more detail than this book does are Beall and van Fraassen 2003, Priest 2008, and Restall 2005. (These three books go over not only the classical theory, which is often the only theory considered by introductory logic textbooks, but also a host of so-called non-classical theories, some of which are sketched in later chapters. As a result, these three books are cited for further reading in many chapters in this book.) Bibliographies in those books point to a (huge) host of alternative sources.

Exercises

1. Show that, on the classical theory, $A \therefore \neg\neg A$ is valid.
2. Show that, according to the classical theory, $A, B \therefore A \wedge B$ is valid.
3. In addition to our definition of *logical truth* (true-in-*every case*), let us define *contingent* and *logically false* as follows.
   - Sentence A is *logically false* iff it is false-in-*every case*.
   - Sentence A is *contingent* iff it is true-in-*some case*, and false-in-*some case*.

   For each of the following sentences of $\mathcal{L}$, say whether, according to the classical theory, it is logically true, logically false, or contingent.[13]

---

[13] Again, for convenience, otherwise requisite parentheses are dropped when confusion won't arise.

(a) $p \rightarrow p$

(b) $p \rightarrow \neg p$

(c) $p \wedge \neg p$

(d) $q \vee p$

(e) $q \wedge (p \vee q)$

(f) $q \vee (p \wedge q)$

(g) $q \leftrightarrow \neg p$

(h) $(p \wedge (p \rightarrow q)) \rightarrow q$

4. For each of the valid forms in §4.7, give a proof that they're valid. (Carefully consider whether there can be a classical case in which the premises are true and the conclusion false. To do this, you'll need to keep going back to the truth conditions for the various connectives. One useful method for doing this is called *Reductio*. The idea, in this context, is to assume that there *is* a counterexample to the given argument, that is, that there *is* a classical case v that satisfies the premises but assigns 0 to the conclusion. If this assumption leads to a contradiction—in particular, that some sentence gets assigned both 1 and 0, which is impossible—you conclude, via Reductio, that the initial assumption was wrong, that is, that there can't, contrary to your initial assumption, be a classical counterexample.)

5. Prove that, where $\vdash$ is our basic classical consequence relation, each of the following are true (i.e., that the given argument forms are valid in the basic classical theory).

(a) $A \rightarrow B, B \rightarrow C \vdash A \rightarrow C$.

(b) $(A \vee B) \wedge C, A \rightarrow \neg C \vdash B$.

(c) $(A \vee B) \wedge C \dashv\vdash (A \wedge C) \vee (B \wedge C)$.

(d) $(A \wedge B) \vee C \dashv\vdash (A \vee C) \wedge (B \vee C)$.

(e) $A \rightarrow B, \neg A \rightarrow B \vdash B$.

6. Suppose that, instead of functions, we model our classical cases as *sets of sentences*. A *case*, on this approach, is a set $\mathcal{X}$ of $\mathcal{L}$ sentences. In turn, we say that *truth in a case* is just membership—i.e., being an element—in such a set. Your task is two-fold:

(a) What constraints do we impose on the given cases for them to be *classical*—i.e., 'complete' and 'consistent'?

  (b) What are the truth conditions for conjunctions, disjunctions, and negations on this approach?

7. Can you think of a way of defining ∨ in terms of ¬ and ∧? (Hint: see whether you can come up with a sentence that uses only ¬ and ∧ but has exactly the same 'truth table' as ∨.) If so, you've shown that, strictly speaking, we can reduce our number of basic connectives to just ¬ and ∧ (and treat ∨, like the others, as defined).

8. Related to the previous question, can you think of a way of defining ∧ in terms of ∨ and ¬?

Sample answers

Answer 3b. The sentence $p \rightarrow \neg p$ is contingent: it is true-in-*some case* and false-in-*some case*. Proof: p is atomic, and so there are cases in which p is true, and also cases in which p is false. Let v be any case in which p is true, that is, $v(p) = 1$. By the classical treatment of negation, $v(\neg p) = 0$. By definition, $p \rightarrow \neg p$ is equivalent to $\neg p \vee \neg p$.[14] By the truth conditions for disjunction, $\neg p \vee \neg p$ is true iff one of its disjuncts is true; but $\neg p$ is the only disjunct, and it is not true-in-the-given-case, since $v(\neg p) = 0$. So, v is a case in which $p \rightarrow \neg p$ is not true. On the other hand, consider any case v' in which p is false, that is, $v'(p) = 0$. By the truth conditions for negation, $v'(\neg p) = 1$, in which case, by the truth conditions for disjunction, $v'(\neg p \vee \neg p) = 1$, and hence $v'(p \rightarrow \neg p) = 1$. So, v' is a case in which $p \rightarrow \neg p$ is true. Hence, there are cases in which $p \rightarrow \neg p$ is true and cases in which it is false.

Answer 4-LEM. To see that LEM is a valid form (i.e., that all of its instances are logically true sentences), we need to show that there's no case in which $A \vee \neg A$ is false (for any sentence A). We do this by Reductio. Suppose, for reductio, that there's some case v such that $v(A \vee \neg A) = 0$ (for some sentence A). The truth conditions for disjunction tell us that $v(A \vee \neg A) = 1$ if and only if $v(A) = 1$ or $v(\neg A) = 1$. Since, by supposition, $v(A \vee \neg A) \neq 1$ (since v is a function which has assigned 0 to $A \vee \neg A$), we have it that $v(A) \neq 1$ and $v(\neg A) \neq 1$. But since v has to assign

---

[14]Recall from §4.6 that $A \rightarrow B$ is defined to be $\neg A \vee B$.

either 1 or 0 to every sentence, we conclude that $v(A) = 0$ and $v(\neg A) = 0$. But this is impossible, since, by truth conditions for negation, $v(\neg A) = 1$ iff $v(A) = 0$. So, we conclude that our initial supposition—namely, that there's some case v in which $A \vee \neg A$ (for some A) is false—is itself untrue. Hence, we conclude that there cannot be a (classical) case in which $A \vee \neg A$ (for some A) is false, which is to say that LEM is valid.

Answer 4-Simplification. To see that $A \wedge B$ implies A in the classical theory, we can use Reductio.[15] Suppose, for reductio, that there's a counterexample to $A \wedge B \therefore A$, that there's some (classical) case v such that $v(A \wedge B) = 1$ but $v(A) = 0$. The truth conditions for conjunction tell us that $v(A \wedge B) = 1$ iff $v(A) = 1$ and $v(B) = 1$. But, then, we have it that $v(A) = 1$, since (by supposition) we have it that $v(A \wedge B) = 1$. But, by supposition, we also have it that $v(A) = 0$. This is impossible, since v is a function and, so, cannot assign anything to *both* 1 and 0. (If you've forgotten the chief feature of functions, you should turn back to Chapter 3 for a quick review!) Hence, we reject our initial assumption that there's a counterexample to Simplification, and conclude that there's no counterexample—and, hence, that the given form is valid.

---

[15]NB: we certainly do not need to use Reductio, since the answer falls directly out of the truth conditions for conjunction; however, it may be useful to give a few examples of Reductio reasoning.

5

A Paracomplete Theory

A hard fact of life is that life is unsettled.
– Max Bealliggins

In this chapter, we briefly explore a variation on the classical theory of our basic connectives. The target theory is a nonclassical *rival* of the classical theory; it agrees with the classical theory on *what* the (basic) logical connectives are, but it disagrees on how they work.

We will begin the discussion with some philosophical motivation (unsettledness), and then turn to an informal characterization of the given theory, and then a brief sketch of the target formal language.

5.1 Apparent unsettledness

Some philosophers have thought that natural languages (e.g., English) are 'unsettled', that they are 'indeterminate' in places, the idea being that some sentences, in some sense, are 'neither true nor false'.

A variety of phenomena motivate such a view of our language. Perhaps the strongest motivation arises from the apparent vagueness of (some fragments of) our language.[1]

Why is it that legal courts stipulate a *legal meaning* for 'child', 'adult', and so on? Why not simply use the ordinary meanings of such terms? The answer is not that such terms are meaningless; rather, such terms are not sufficiently settled over all cases. Because matters of law require—or, at least, strive towards—precision, courts simply stipulate a new word (say, 'child*'), one with precise meaning to take the place of our otherwise vague

---

[1]I should note that there is much controversy over how, exactly, *vagueness* is to be characterized. What follows is a very simplified, and very limited, discussion.

words. Of course, wise courts try to preserve the original, ordinary meanings as far the meanings go (e.g., they don't declare that a 91 year old man is a legal child); however, they stipulate a new, precise (or more precise) term for legal matters.

The ordinary meaning of 'child' (or the like) is settled with respect to *some* objects, in the sense that 'child' is true of some objects and false of others; however, there are some objects of which 'child' seems neither true nor false. To see such unsettledness, simply consider the following task.

- Task: figure out exactly when—that is, at what precise moment—you ceased being a child!

The task is seemingly impossible to carry out, unless you substitute some precise sense of 'child' (e.g., a stipulated legal sense) for the intended, ordinary meaning. At one time, you were clearly a child, but now you are not. At the former time(s), 'child' was true of you; at the latter time(s), 'child' was false of you. The unsettledness is apparent when you consider the 'in-between' stages, what philosophers sometimes call the *borderline region*. In this example, the borderline comprises those times at which 'child' is neither true nor false of you; it's the region over which the ordinary meaning of the term is unsettled.[2]

The relevant sense of 'unsettledness', whatever exactly it might be, is not an *epistemic* sense.[3] We aren't *ignorant* of the precise meaning of 'child', but rather the ordinary meaning is not fully precise and fully exhaustive. The ordinary meaning of 'child' doesn't exhaustively cover all objects; it fails to exhaustively divide objects into those of which 'child' is true and those of which 'child' is false. Instead, the ordinary meaning seems to leave *gaps*: there seem to be some objects such that the predicate 'child' neither definitely applies nor definitely fails to apply. In some—non-

---

[2]If the term 'child' is not a good example, try the same task with the term 'short'. At what exact moment did you cease to be short? (Of course, you can *stipulate* a precise meaning for 'short', e.g. less than n feet in height, but that's not the task.)

[3]Some philosophers think that it is an epistemic sense. They think that our language is entirely precise, but that we're somehow unable—*in principle* unable—to fully know the precise meanings of our language. For present purposes, such epistemicist views will be set aside, despite the interesting issues that such views raise.

epistemic—sense, the matter is simply unsettled; there's 'no fact of the matter' one way or the other.

The ancient *sorites* puzzle (pronounced 'so-*right*-tees') is often invoked to highlight the apparent unsettledness of (much of) our language. Consider the following argument.

p1. 1 grain of sand is not a heap (of sand).

p2. If 1 grain of sand is not a heap, then 2 grains is not a heap.

p3. If 2 grains of sand is not a heap, then 3 grains is not a heap.

p4. If 3 grains of sand is not a heap, then 4 grains is not a heap.

$\vdots$

c. Therefore, a billion zillion grains of sand is not a heap.

The ordinary meaning of 'heap' is such that a small difference makes no difference in its application. Adding only one grain of sand to something that is definitely not a heap does not suddenly produce a heap of sand. This is the import of the conditional premises.

The trouble, at least for the classical theory, is that the above argument is valid according to the classical theory. If we let p_n be 'n many grains of sand makes a heap of sand' (and letting $\star$ be our 'billion zillion' number), then the above argument can be rewritten with the following form (using our defined connective, the conditional).

$\neg p_1$

$\neg p_1 \rightarrow \neg p_2$

$\neg p_2 \rightarrow \neg p_3$

$\neg p_3 \rightarrow \neg p_4$

$\vdots$

$\neg p_\star$

As you can check, this is valid in the basic classical theory.

If the above argument is *sound*, then we must conclude that there are no heaps of sand at all. (If you don't care about heaps of sand, just run the same sorites for *children* and moments of time or etc.) On the other hand, if (p1) is true but one of the conditionals is false, then the classical theory saddles us with something very difficult to believe: namely, that exactly one grain of sand makes all the difference between a heap and a non-heap.

One response to the sorites is that the classical theory gets things wrong. This is not surprising. The classical theory is motivated by the idea of a *precise* language. If, as the foregoing suggests, our language has pockets of imprecision—that is, meaningful but nonetheless unsettled sentences—then the classical theory is too narrow for an account of consequence in our broader language.

Such unsettledness, at least on the surface, seems to motivate a *broadening* of our logical theory. We will look at a natural such broadening, a non-classical logical theory that is motivated by apparent 'unsettledness'.[4]

5.2   Cases: incomplete

What the foregoing considerations motivate is not a rejection of classical cases; rather, such considerations motivate a *broadening* of our account of cases. In addition to complete and consistent cases (as per Chapter 4), considerations of 'unsettledness' motivate *incomplete* cases, cases in which, for some A, neither A nor $\neg A$ is true.

We will use the term 'paracomplete' for any logical theory that recognizes *incomplete* cases—cases in which, for some A, neither A nor $\neg A$ is true.

Definition 29. (Paracomplete) *A logical theory is* paracomplete *if it recognizes a case c such that $c \not\models_1 A$ and $c \not\models_1 \neg A$, for some sentence A.*

The term 'paracomplete' comes from the Greek word 'para' for *beyond*, the idea being that we're moving beyond having only 'complete cases'.

In principle, one could certainly advocate a paracomplete theory according to which *all* cases are incomplete; however, the motivation for such a theory is not clear. For our purposes, we will focus on a fairly conservative paracomplete theory, one that *retains* all classical cases, but simply moves beyond the classical cases by also recognizing incomplete cases.

---

[4]I should note that I'm not giving an historically accurate account of the motivation behind this chapter's logical theory. Still, the given logical theory—so-called (basic) Strong Kleene—is often thought to be a natural first thought about how our unsettled language and its logic might work.

In short, then, *paracomplete cases* are either *complete and consistent* (i.e., classical cases) or *incomplete and consistent*. Hence, since classical cases are complete and consistent, any classical case counts as a paracomplete case. On the other hand, some paracomplete cases—namely, the incomplete ones—are not classical. So, the paracomplete theory expands the classical account of cases; it retains classical cases, but adds another type of case, namely, incomplete and consistent cases.

5.3 Paracomplete truth and falsity conditions

The philosophical picture behind our paracomplete theory has it that some sentences—some meaningful, declarative sentences—are 'neither true nor false'. Such 'unsettled sentences', according to a common metaphor, are *gaps*; they fall into the 'gap' between truth and falsity. Metaphor aside, the important point is that such 'gaps' are not meaningless; they are meaningful sentences that, for whatever reason, simply fail to be either true or false.

What, now, are the truth conditions (i.e., truth-in-a-case conditions) for our given connectives—the same 'basic connectives' (plus defined connectives) from Chapter 4? A natural idea, which we will pursue, is—in effect—to *retain the same truth conditions for molecular sentences*; the only change occurs in the truth conditions for atomics.

5.3.1 *Atomics and Falsity*

Recall that, in Chapter 4, we didn't really give explicit truth conditions for atomic sentences. Instead, we simply stipulated the following *classical constraint*.

- *Classical Constraint for Atomics.* For any *atomic A* and any case c, either $c \models_1 A$ or $c \models_1 \neg A$.

Given the definition of 'complete case' (from Chapter 4), this amounts to saying that any case is complete with respect to atomic A, which is certainly right for the classical theory.

In the current, paracomplete theory, we should drop the classical constraint on atomics. After all, the main paracomplete idea is that there are cases that are incomplete with respect to atomic A, that is, cases c such that $c \not\models_1 A$ and $c \not\models_1 \neg A$. The question is: what constraint on atomics should be imposed for the paracomplete theory?

Unfortunately, an issue concerning *falsity*—or, more accurately, *falsity in a case*—arises at this stage. Recall that, with classical cases, we said that A is *false-in-c* iff $c \models_1 \neg A$, and that $c \models_1 \neg A$ iff $c \not\models_1 A$ (i.e., $\neg A$ is true-in-c iff A is *untrue* or *not* true-in-c). This is *not* accurate for our paracomplete cases.

For our paracomplete theory, we retain the classical idea that A is false-in-c iff $c \models_1 \neg A$ (i.e., a sentence is false-in-a-case iff its negation is true-in-that-case). The trouble, however, is that *untruth* and *falsity* come apart in the paracomplete logical theory. On one hand, our paracomplete theory maintains, as above, that cases are consistent; hence, for all sentences A and all paracomplete cases c, if $c \models_1 \neg A$ then $c \not\models_1 A$. On the other hand, as above, our paracomplete theory acknowledges cases that are entirely incomplete with respect to A, that is, some case c such that $c \not\models_1 A$ and $c \not\models_1 \neg A$, for some A. Accordingly, on the paracomplete theory, we can have some A and some case c such that $c \not\models_1 A$, but this does *not* mean that $c \models_1 \neg A$. The upshot is that we can no longer define *false-in-a-case* to be *not true-in-a-case*, at least for the paracomplete theory.

How, then, are we to understand *false-in-a-case* for the paracomplete theory? The answer, in part, can be given if we were to spell out the explicit truth (and falsity!) conditions for atomic sentences.[5] We won't do that in this chapter. Instead, we will simply assume that, for any paracomplete case c, every atomic A is either true-in-c, false-in-c, or neither true-in-c nor false-in-c.

To make things clearer, let us slightly change our notation to accommodate the broader, paracomplete theory. In particular, let us continue to use '$c \models_1 A$' to abbreviate 'A is true-in-c', but now also use '$c \models_0 A$' to abbreviate 'A is false-in-c'. While we still won't give explicit truth (or falsity!) conditions for atomics (at least in this chapter), we will give the following constraint on *atomics*.

---

[5] For convenience, the term 'truth conditions' (or, more accurately, 'truth-in-a-case conditions'), unless otherwise stated, will henceforth be shorthand for 'truth and falsity conditions' (or, again, for 'truth-in-a-case and falsity-in-a-case conditions').

- *Paracomplete Constraint for Atomics.* For any *atomic A* and any case *c*, exactly one of the following obtains.

  $c \models_1 A$ and $c \not\models_0 A$

  $c \not\models_1 A$ and $c \models_0 A$

  $c \not\models_1 A$ and $c \not\models_0 A$

For present purposes, we don't need to know *how* atomics get to be true-in-a-case or false-in-a-case; we just need to know that, for any (paracomplete) case c, every atomic is either true-in-c, false-in-c, or neither true-in-c nor false-in-c.

5.3.2 *Molecular sentences*

With the paracomplete constraint for atomics, we can give truth-in-a-paracomplete-case conditions for molecular sentences. There are various options one might pursue for such truth conditions.[6] What is different, in the paracomplete case, is that, in addition to giving truth conditions, we must also explicitly give *falsity conditions*—we must specify the conditions under which sentences are false in a given case. The reason for this is that, as noted above, falsity and untruth come apart in the paracomplete case. As such, from $c \not\models_1 A$ we cannot infer $c \models_0 A$.

For present purposes, we will stick as closely to the *classical* truth conditions (see Chapter 4) as possible.

Definition 30. (Basic Paracomplete Truth and Falsity Conditions) *Where c is any case, and A and B any sentences of $\mathcal{L}$,[7] the paracomplete conditions for the basic connectives are as follows.*

Conjunction: $c \models_1 A \wedge B$ *if and only if* $c \models_1 A$ *and* $c \models_1 B$.

Conjunction: $c \models_0 A \wedge B$ *if and only if* $c \models_0 A$ *or* $c \models_0 B$.

Disjunction: $c \models_1 A \vee B$ *if and only if* $c \models_1 A$ *or* $c \models_1 B$.

Disjunction: $c \models_0 A \vee B$ *if and only if* $c \models_0 A$ *and* $c \models_0 B$.

Negation: $c \models_1 \neg A$ *if and only if* $c \models_0 A$.

Negation: $c \models_0 \neg A$ *if and only if* $c \models_1 A$.[8]

---

[6]See exercises (concerning 'Weak Kleene'), and also Chapter 12!

[7]As in the previous chapter, $\mathcal{L}$ is a language with only the basic connectives of conjunction, disjunction, and negation.

[8]Note: given these conditions on negation, the paracomplete constraint on atomics (see §5.3.1) yields exactly one of the following for any paracomplete

This tells us that, according to the paracomplete theory, a conjunction is true-in-a-case just if both conjuncts are true-in-that-case, and a conjunction is false-in-a-case just if one of the conjuncts is false; otherwise, the conjunction is neither true- nor false-in-the-given-case (i.e., it is gappy). Similarly, a disjunction is true-in-a-case iff at least one of the disjuncts is true-in-the-case, and false-in-a-case iff both disjuncts are false-in-the-case; otherwise, it is gappy in the given case. Finally, we have it that a negation is true-in-a-case just if the negatum is false-in-the-given-case, and false-in-the-given-case just if the negatum is true-in-the-given-case; otherwise, the negation is gappy in the given case.

What is important to observe is that the foregoing conditions are simply the basic classical truth conditions, except that the cases are now paracomplete (and, so, needn't be complete). In particular, notice that the given falsity conditions, which are redundant in the classical theory (why?), are exactly the conditions under which sentences are false-in-classical cases. If you think about it, this shouldn't be surprising, since, as above, our paracomplete theory simply *expands* the range of cases beyond the classical ones; it does *not* remove any of the classical cases.

In effect, the classical theory is what you get from the paracomplete theory if you ignore incomplete cases. As such, the classical theory might be seen as a narrow version of the paracomplete.

5.4   Paracomplete consequence

As per Chapter 1, B is a consequence of A iff there's no case in which A is true but B not true. In the present approach, cases are *paracomplete cases*, which are either classical cases or incomplete but consistent cases. Given the truth (and falsity) conditions above, we can see a few notable features of the paracomplete consequence relation.

---

case c and any sentence A.

$c \models_1 A$ and $c \not\models_1 \neg A$
$c \not\models_1 A$ and $c \models_1 \neg A$
$c \not\models_1 A$ and $c \not\models_1 \neg A$

5.4.1   *Paracomplete and classical consequence*

Let us use '$\vdash_{bc}$' for *basic classical consequence* and '$\vdash_{K3}$' for our given *basic paracomplete consequence* relation.[9] One notable fact about the relation between the two consequence relations—namely, the basic classical and basic paracomplete relations—is the following.

> CP. Let $\mathcal{X}$ be any set of $\mathcal{L}$ sentences, and A any sentence of $\mathcal{L}$.
> Fact: if $\mathcal{X} \vdash_{K3} A$ then $\mathcal{X} \vdash_{bc} A$.

To see this, recall that consequence is absence of counterexample—that is, absence of any (relevant) case in which the premises are true but conclusion not true. So, suppose $\mathcal{X} \vdash_{K3} A$, that is, that there's no paracomplete case in which everything in $\mathcal{X}$ is true but A not true. Any classical case is a paracomplete case, since paracomplete cases, by definition, are either classical cases or incomplete but consistent cases. Hence, since there's no paracomplete case that serves as a counterexample to the argument from $\mathcal{X}$ to A, there's thereby no classical case that serves as a counterexample to the argument, which means that $\mathcal{X} \vdash_{bc} A$.

CP tells us something important about the relation between our basic classical consequence relation and our broader paracomplete consequence relation: namely, that the latter is a *proper part* of the former. In other words, the basic classical consequence relation is 'stronger' than the broader paracomplete one; however, the former has the latter as a proper part—a 'sub-relation'. CP tells us that any arguments that are valid according to the paracomplete theory are valid according to the classical theory. As it turns out, the converse doesn't hold; there are some arguments—mainly, involving logical truths—that are valid according to the classical theory but not the paracomplete theory. The reason is that the latter theory recognizes more cases than the classical theory, and hence recognizes more 'potential counterexamples'.

Philosophically, CP suggests that, while our language may have an 'unsettled' or 'gappy' fragment, it may also enjoy an en-

---

[9]We use 'bc' for *basic classical*. The name 'K3' is standard for our basic paracomplete consequence relation. The K3 relation (or, generally, logical theory) is so called for the logician Stephen Kleene's most famous 3-valued logic, namely, our current basic paracomplete logic under discussion. (The given paracomplete theory is also sometimes called *Strong Kleene*.)

tirely precise, classical fragment. For example, it might be that the mathematical or scientific fragment of our language is precise and, in effect, classical, even though our broader language—perhaps due to a bit of vague language or the like—is 'unsettled' or 'gappy'. (How does CP suggest as much? This question is left as an exercise.)

5.4.2 *Absence of logical truths*

Another notable feature of the basic paracomplete theory is that, contrary to the classical theory, there are no logical truths! Recall that, in general, A is a logical truth iff A is true-in-*all cases*. On the paracomplete theory, our cases are either classical *or* incomplete but consistent. As above, the paracomplete theory has a broader range of cases than the classical theory. The result of such broadening is that there are more 'potential counterexamples'.

Of course, given the philosophical motivation of the paracomplete theory—for example, *unsettledness* or *gaps*—one would expect that Excluded Middle would fail, and it does. To see this, recall that Excluded Middle fails if there's a case in which $A \vee \neg A$ is not true. On the paracomplete theory, there is certainly such a case. After all, just consider a case c that is incomplete with respect to A, that is, a case c such that $c \not\models_1 A$ and $c \not\models_0 A$. By the given truth conditions for negation (see §5.3.2), we have it that if $c \not\models_0 A$ then $c \not\models_1 \neg A$. Hence, in our given case c, we have it that $c \not\models_1 A$ and $c \not\models_1 \neg A$. But, then, by the truth condition for disjunction, we have it that $c \not\models_1 A \vee \neg A$ (since neither disjunct is true-in-c). Hence, there is a paracomplete case in which $A \vee \neg A$ is not true. Hence, Excluded Middle is not a logically true (sentence) form, according to our paracomplete theory.

That there are *no* logical truths, on the paracomplete theory, is slightly more difficult to see (until we get to the formal picture, below). The basic idea, however, is that there is a paracomplete case—namely, an incomplete but consistent case—in which every *atomic* A is neither true nor false. With suitable attention to the truth and falsity conditions for molecular sentences (see §5.3.2), one can see that such a case will be one in which *no* sentence—atomic or molecular—is true or false. Hence, there is a case in which *no* sentence is true, and so no sentence is true in *all* cases—and, hence, there are no logical truths. This result, as said, will be easier to see in the formal picture, to which we now turn.

5.5   Formal picture

As throughout, the main aim of a logical theory is to specify the consequence relation of a given language. As in Chapter 4, we are concentrating on a language with only a few basic connectives, and we are ignoring any structure within our atomic sentences. Our aim in this section is to briefly sketch a formal picture of our given paracomplete logical theory of such a language. Towards that end, we will give a sketch of a formal language, a sketch of the semantics (viz., truth conditions) for the language, and then define the consequence relation on the given language. What follows, as in Chapter 4, presupposes the set-theoretic tools that you learned in Chapter 3.

5.5.1   *Syntax*

The syntax of our language $\mathcal{L}$ is exactly the same as in Chapter 4. The difference between the classical and paracomplete accounts of $\mathcal{L}$ arises at the level of semantics.

5.5.2   *Semantics*

As you know by now, the key ingredients of logical consequence are *cases* and *truth-in-a-case* (and *falsity-in-a-case*) conditions. Our concern, in this chapter, is with a basic paracomplete theory. The question is: how shall we model our paracomplete cases?

There are various ways of modeling our given (paracomplete) cases. We will stick to an approach that is similar to the approach taken towards modeling classical cases. In particular, we will take our cases to be (modeled by) certain functions—ones obeying various constraints—from our set $\mathcal{S}$ of sentences into our set $\mathcal{V}$ of 'semantic values'. (See Chapter 4 for the classical approach.) What's *different*, now, is that we will *expand* our set of 'semantic values' from $\{1, 0\}$ to $\{1, n, 0\}$ (where 'n' may be thought to mark the semantic status of being *neither true nor false*). The idea, intuitively, is that the paracomplete theory retains the classical semantic values; however, it also recognizes more options—namely, an 'unsettledness' or 'gappy' semantic value. Intuitively, one can think of the value n as marking 'unsettled' or 'gappy' sentences, the idea being that if A is assigned n in a case, then, intuitively, it is 'unsettled' or 'gappy' in that case.

To be clearer, our semantics begins with a set of semantic values, namely, $\mathcal{V} = \{1, \mathsf{n}, 0\}$.[10] In turn, we let our *cases* be functions v from $\mathcal{S}$ into $\mathcal{V}$, so that we have $v(A) = 1$ or $v(A) = \mathsf{n}$ or $v(A) = 0$ for every sentence A and any such case v.

As with the classical language, let us define *truth in a case* as follows: A is *true-in-a-case* v (remember that our 'cases' are now functions) if and only if $v(A) = 1$. Similarly, A is *false-in-a-case* v if and only if $v(A) = 0$.

Notice that, as in the classical language, we do *not* want to allow just *any* old function from $\mathcal{S}$ into $\mathcal{V}$ to count as a classical case! After all, there are certainly functions from $\mathcal{S}$ into $\mathcal{V}$ that do not respect the paracomplete truth conditions (see §5.3.2). Consider, for example, a function v such that $v(A \wedge \neg A) = 1$. This is certainly a function from $\mathcal{S}$ into $\mathcal{V}$, but it doesn't respect the intended consistency of paracomplete cases. Paracomplete cases are consistent, and so we don't want to have a case v such that $v(A \wedge \neg A) = 1$.

Following the pattern in Chapter 4, we rule out such 'unwanted' functions from our set of cases by invoking the following truth conditions. In particular, we say that a function v, from $\mathcal{S}$ into $\mathcal{V}$, is a *paracomplete case* if and only if it 'obeys' the following truth conditions—this time, given entirely in tables.

$\neg$		$\wedge$	1	n	0		$\vee$	1	n	0
0	1	1	1	1	n	0	1	1	1	1
n	n	n	n	n	n	0	n	1	n	n
1	0	0	0	0	0	0	0	1	n	0

In effect, such conditions, represented in the tables, reflect a fairly classical approach to 'unsettledness'. For example, a negation is true just if its negatum is false, and it's false just if the negatum is true—just as in the classical picture. The difference, of course,

---

[10]When one's semantic values go beyond two, the given language is called a *many-valued language*. In such semantics, one usually talks about a subset $\mathcal{D}$ of $\mathcal{V}$, where $\mathcal{D}$ contains the so-called *designated values*—the values in terms of which validity or consequence is defined. This will be important in the next chapter, but we'll sidestep this terminology here.

is that the negatum might be neither true nor false, in which case the condition (above) tells us that the negation itself is neither true nor false. Similarly, a disjunction is true iff at least one of the disjuncts is true; it is false iff both disjuncts are false. This is exactly as things are in the classical picture. The difference is that, in the paracomplete picture, a disjunct might be neither true nor false, in which case, the disjunction is neither true nor false if the other disjunct fails to be true. conjunctions are similarly 'classical' in spirit, as you can check.

The final step, in giving the semantics, is to specify our target relation: namely, logical consequence. The definition is just an instance of our recipe in Chapter 1.

Definition 31. (Basic Paracomplete Consequence) *B is a logical consequence of A if and only if there is no paracomplete case v such that $v(A) = 1$ but $v(B) \neq 1$.*

To make this more general, let us say that v *satisfies* a sentence A iff $v(A) = 1$ (i.e., iff A is true-in-the-given-case). In turn, let $\mathcal{X}$ be any set of $\mathcal{L}$ sentences. We say that v *satisfies* $\mathcal{X}$ iff v satisfies every member of $\mathcal{X}$. With this terminology, we can give a more general definition of basic paracomplete consequence (instead of only single-premise arguments), which, as above, we'll officially represent as $\vdash_{K3}$ but often just write as $\vdash$ when it is clear that we are talking about our given paracomplete relation).

Definition 32. (General Basic Paracomplete Consequence) $\mathcal{X} \vdash A$ *iff there is no paracomplete case v that satisfies $\mathcal{X}$ but not A.*

You should think about this definition, compare it with the 'general recipe' of logical consequence and the classical account, and also evaluate various argument forms for (basic paracomplete) validity. Note that a paracomplete *counterexample* need not be a case in which the conclusion is *false*; it need only be a case in which the conclusion is not true (i.e., assigned anything other than 1).

5.6 Defined connectives

As in Chapter 4, we can introduce various defined connectives. We will use the same defined connectives here, letting '$A \to B$' be shorthand for $\neg A \vee B$, and similarly letting '$A \leftrightarrow B$' be shorthand for $(A \to B) \land (B \to A)$. As in Chapter 4, the truth conditions for these defined connectives are simply the resulting truth conditions for the corresponding sentences that use only our Basic (primitive) connectives—for example, the truth conditions for $\neg A \lor B$ and $(\neg A \lor B) \land (\neg B \lor A)$. In our given paracomplete setting, the given conditions are represented in the following tables.

$\to$	1	n	0		$\leftrightarrow$	1	n	0
1	1	n	0		1	1	n	0
n	1	n	n		n	n	n	n
0	1	1	1		0	0	n	1

5.7 Some notable forms

As in Chapter 4, any logical theory of a language provides an account of the (logical) behavior of the language's connectives. In part, a theory of the connectives is largely reflected in the theory's given truth conditions for the connectives, and the associated account of 'cases'. Still, where the behavior is manifest is in the consequence relation, in particular, the valid argument forms involving those connectives.

We saw, above (see §5.4.1), that our basic paracomplete consequence relation is a 'sub-relation' of the basic classical consequence relation. We also saw that there are no logical truths according to the paracomplete theory. By way of comparing the two theories, recall that *all* of the following forms are classically valid; however, you'll see that some of them (marked by $\nvdash_{K3}$) are not valid according to the paracomplete theory.

- Excluded Middle: $\nvdash_{K3} A \lor \neg A$
- Non-Contradiction: $\nvdash_{K3} \neg(A \land \neg A)$
- Modus Ponens: $A \to B, A \vdash_{K3} B$
- Modus Tollens: $A \to B, \neg B \vdash_{K3} \neg A$
- Disjunctive Syllogism: $A \lor B, \neg A \vdash_{K3} B$
- Contraposition: $A \to B \dashv\vdash_{K3} \neg B \to \neg A$
- Explosion: $A, \neg A \vdash_{K3} B$
- Addition: $A \vdash_{K3} A \lor B$
- Adjunction: $A, B \vdash_{K3} A \land B$
- Simplification: $A \land B \vdash_{K3} A$

- De Morgan: $\neg(A \vee B) \dashv\vdash_{K3} \neg A \wedge \neg B$
- De Morgan: $\neg(A \wedge B) \dashv\vdash_{K3} \neg A \vee \neg B$
- Double Negation: $\neg\neg A \dashv\vdash_{K3} A$

You should prove, using the formal account (and especially formal truth conditions), that the given argument forms are indeed valid. (Use the techniques that you used in Chapter 4, but be sure to consider all semantic values involved in the paracomplete language.)

5.8   Summary and looking ahead

Summary. Motivated by apparent 'unsettledness', our basic paracomplete theory broadens the classical theory's range of cases. In particular, the paracomplete theory agrees that all of the classical cases—namely, all complete and consistent cases—should be among our cases; however, the paracomplete theory, motivated by apparent 'unsettledness', calls for more cases, namely, incomplete but consistent cases. Except for additional such cases, the paracomplete theory agrees with the classical truth conditions and falsity conditions for the basic connectives. The paracomplete approach is modeled by using three semantic values (intuitively, true, false, and gappy), and its cases are functions from sentences into the semantic values—in particular, all and only those functions that 'obey' the appropriate truth (and falsity) conditions. Logical consequence, in turn, is specified as per Chapter 1, but now letting our cases be such (paracomplete) cases and *truth in a case* and *falsity in a case* being defined as having value 1 and 0 (in the given case), respectively. The resulting paracomplete consequence relation enjoys the classical consequence relation as special case: the latter is what you get when you ignore 'incomplete' cases—formally, when you ignore the value n. One significant difference between the two consequence relations is that the former has no logical truths—no sentences true in all (paracomplete) cases.

Looking Ahead. Whether our given paracomplete theory is the best way to model unsettledness (and its logic) is an open philosophical question. For our purposes, the theory gives a natural example of a non-classical 'rival' to the classical logical theory, one motivated by phenomena that, on the surface, are ignored by the classical theory. In the next chapter, we'll look at another rival to both the classical theory and given paracomplete theory, one that is motivated by other phenomena in our language.

Further Reading. For excellent, though somewhat advanced, discussions of 'indeterminacy' and 'vagueness', see Hyde 2008, Keefe and Smith 1997, Smith 2008, Williamson 1994, and the bibliographies therein. For further discussion of (and suitable proof systems for) our target paracomplete theory, see any of Beall and van Fraassen 2003, Priest 2008, and Restall 2005. (As mentioned in the previous chapter, these three books give a more advanced but closely related discussion of logical theories sketched in this book. Their bibliographies can be consulted for a much broader range of sources.)

Exercises

1. Answer any questions raised in the text.
2. We noted that Excluded Middle is not a logically true (sentence) form in the paracomplete theory. Question: is there any case in which $A \vee \neg A$ is *false*? If so, give such a case. If not, say why not.
3. Recall, from Chapter 4, our definitions of *logically true, logically false*, and *contingent*, where A is any sentence.

   - A is *logically true* iff it is true-in-*every case*.
   - A is *logically false* iff it is false-in-*every case*.
   - A is *contingent* iff it is true-in-*some case*, and false-in-*some case*.

   Our given paracomplete theory, as above, has no logical truths. Give a (paracomplete) counterexample to each of the following sentences (i.e., a paracomplete case in which the sentence is *not true*). In addition, specify which, if any, of the following sentences are logically false, and which are contingent.

   (a) $p \rightarrow p$
   (b) $p \rightarrow \neg p$
   (c) $p \wedge \neg p$
   (d) $q \vee p$

(e) $q \wedge (p \vee q)$
(f) $q \vee (p \wedge q)$
(g) $q \leftrightarrow \neg p$
(h) $(p \wedge (p \rightarrow q)) \rightarrow q$
(i) $p \vee \neg p$
(j) $\neg(p \wedge \neg p)$

4. Suppose that we define a different, broader sort of 'contingency' thus:

- A sentence A is *broadly contingent* iff it is true-in-*some case* and *not* true-in-*some case* (i.e., *untrue*-in-some case).

  Which, if any, of the displayed sentences (3a)–(3j), from exercise 3, are broadly contingent? Also: in the given paracomplete theory, can a sentence be broadly contingent without being contingent?

5. By way of contrast, redo exercises 3 and 4 above in terms of the *classical* theory.

6. For each of the valid forms in §5.7, give a proof that they're valid.

7. *Weak Kleene.* An alternative paracomplete theory, one that is less classical than the one in this chapter, is so-called Weak Kleene (WK). On this approach, cases are as in our given paracomplete theory; however, the truth- and falsity-in-a-case conditions differ quite a bit with respect to the 'gappy' value n. In particular, the truth and falsity conditions are the same as our given paracomplete theory with respect to the *classical values* (i.e., 1 and 0); however, the conditions concerning n are as follows. If, for some WK case v, we have it that either $v(A) = \mathsf{n}$ or $v(B) = \mathsf{n}$, then $v(\neg A) = \mathsf{n} = v(\neg B)$, and similarly $v(A \vee B) = \mathsf{n} = v(A \wedge B)$. On this approach, any whiff of 'unsettledness' in a (molecular) sentence renders the entire sentence gappy (or unsettled). The question: what, if any, of the argument forms in §5.7 are valid on the WK logical theory? (Consequence, for the WK theory, is defined as usual, where *truth in a case* and *falsity in a case* are defined as per our given paracomplete theory in terms of 1 and 0, respectively.)

Sample answers

Answer 3i. The sentence $p \lor \neg p$ fits into none of our given categories: it's not logically true; it's not logically false; and it's not contingent. To establish this, we address each claim in turn.

3i.a. $p \lor \neg p$ is not logically true, as there are cases in which it is not true. In particular, let v be any (paracomplete) case in which p is gappy, that is, $v(p) = $ n. By the truth conditions for negation (see the table in §5.5.2), $v(\neg p) = $ n. By the truth conditions for disjunction, $v(p \lor \neg p) = $ n. Hence, any case in which p is gappy is one in which $p \lor \neg p$ is gappy, and so untrue.

3i.b. $p \lor \neg p$ is not logically false, as there are cases in which it is not false. In particular, see the case above in (3i.a).

3i.c. $p \lor \neg p$ is not contingent, as there is *no* paracomplete case in which it is false. To see this, note that $v(p \lor \neg p) = 0$ iff $v(p) = 0 = v(\neg p)$; but the truth conditions for negation require that $v(p) \neq v(\neg p)$.

Answer 4i. $p \lor \neg p$ is broadly contingent. There are cases in which it is true: for example, any case v such that $v(p) = 1$ or $v(p) = 0$ is one in which $v(p \lor \neg p) = 1$. (Why?) Moreover, there are cases in which $p \lor \neg p$ is not true: let v be any case such that $v(p) = $ n.

6

A Paraconsistent Theory

> *Contradiction is not a sign of falsity,*
> *nor the lack of contradiction a sign of truth.*
> – Blaise Pascal

In the last chapter, we expanded our range of cases to include incomplete but consistent cases. In this chapter, we look at a logical theory that is a rival to both the classical and basic paracomplete theories. As before, the target theory agrees with the preceding theories on *what* the (basic) logical connectives are, but it disagrees on how they work.

We will begin the discussion with some philosophical motivation (overdeterminacy), and then turn to an informal characterization of the given theory, and then a brief sketch of the target formal language.

6.1 Apparent overdeterminacy

In addition to indeterminacy, briefly discussed in the last chapter, some philosophers have thought that our language also exhibits *overdeterminacy*. A sentence is said to be overdetermined if it is both true and false. Falsity, as in previous chapters, is truth of negation: a sentence A is false iff its negation $\neg A$ is true. So, to say that a sentence is overdetermined is to say that it is true *and* that its negation is true.

Are there such sentences in our language? The question is controversial, but we will look at a simple example, namely, the Liar paradox. Before getting to the paradox, we first need to say something about truth.

Truth is often thought to work as follows. If a sentence is true, then what it says is the case.[1] Moreover, if what a sentence

---

[1] This is a different usage of 'case', of course, than we've used in previous chapters.

says is the case, then the sentence is true. For example, if 'Agnes is sleeping' is true, then Agnes is sleeping. In turn, if Agnes is sleeping, then 'Agnes is sleeping' is true. Such features of truth can be made formally precise in a richer language than we're currently considering, but the idea, as sketched, should be clear enough for present purposes.

Now, our language is very resourceful. It can be used to say interesting things, beautiful things, funny things, and boring things. In addition, the language can be used to say paradoxical things. Consider, in particular, the following, starred sentence—an example of the famous Liar paradox.

$\star$ The starred sentence on page 81 of §6.1 of *Logic: The Basics* is false.

Is the starred sentence true? Well, if it is true, then what it says is the case. What it says is that it is false. Hence, if the starred sentence is true, then it is false. On the other hand, if the starred sentence is false, then it speaks truly (since it says that it is false), and hence is true. So, if the starred sentence is false, it is true. Putting all of this together, we see that the starred sentence is true if and only if it is false.

What we seem to have, then, is a sentence which is both true and false! In both the classical and our basic paracomplete theory (of Chapter 5), this is impossible. Such a sentence would require an inconsistent case, and neither of our previous theories allows for such a thing.

What you might be thinking is that there's really no problem here. After all, we have already expanded our cases to involve incomplete cases. (See Chapter 5.) In doing so, we have rejected Excluded Middle; we've rejected the idea that *every* sentence is true or false. Why can't we simply say that the starred sentence is another case of 'indeterminacy', a 'gappy' sentence that is neither true nor false? If we do, then the argument that it is *both* true and false breaks down.

Such a thought is correct, but the problem lingers. Suppose that we say, as suggested, that the starred sentence is gappy (i.e., neither true nor false). This gets around inconsistency with the starred sentence, but our language has other such sentences. Consider, in particular, the ticked sentence.

✓ The ticked sentence on page 81 of §6.1 of *Logic: The Basics* is either false or it's gappy.

Saying that the ticked sentence is gappy implies that it is true! After all, a disjunction, at least on the theories we're considering, is true iff at least one disjunct is true. Hence, if the ticked sentence is gappy, then one of its disjuncts is true. Similarly, if the sentence is false, then the other disjunct is true, and so the ticked sentence is true. Either way, we seem to have more inconsistency.

The foregoing considerations might not convince you that our language admits of overdeterminacy. Still, the Liar paradox, and related such phenomena, have motivated the idea of inconsistent cases, to which we turn.

6.2   Cases: inconsistent

What the foregoing considerations motivate is not a rejection of classical cases or, more generally, paracomplete cases. Such considerations motivate a *broadening* of our account of cases. In addition to our classical and paracomplete cases, considerations of overdeterminacy motivate *inconsistent* cases, cases in which, for some A, *both A and $\neg A$ are true*.

For convenience, let us introduce a special sort of case, namely, the so-called *trivial case*.

Definition 33. (Trivial Case) *A case c is said to be* trivial *if and only if* all *sentences (of the given language) are true in the case.*

For the basic language that we've been considering—with only disjunction, conjunction, negation, and defined connectives—any trivial case will be both *complete* and *inconsistent*, but it will also be 'overly complete' and 'overly inconsistent'. In particular, any trivial case c, given the definition above, is such that both A and $\neg A$ are true in c, for *all* sentences A.[2] The trivial case, to say the least, is wildly strange.

What is worth noting is that in both the classical and (our previous) paracomplete theories, Explosion holds: $A, \neg A \vdash B$. According to those theories, then, if there's some case in which both A and $\neg A$ are true, then that case is the trivial case. (Why?)

---

[2]Notice that, for any given language, there's exactly one trivial case. Why?

We will use the term 'paraconsistent' for any logical theory that recognizes *inconsistent but non-trivial* cases—cases in which, for *some A*, both *A* and ¬*A* are true, but not *all A* are true.

Definition 34. (Paraconsistent) *A logical theory is paraconsistent if it recognizes some case c such that c* ⊨₁ *A and c* ⊨₁ ¬*A, for some A, but also c* ⊭₁ *B, for some B.*

The term 'paraconsistent', like 'paracomplete', comes from the Greek word 'para' for *beyond*, the idea now being that we're moving beyond having only 'consistent cases'.

Of course, a paraconsistent theory might recognize *only* inconsistent cases (at least some of which are non-trivial), but the motivation for such a theory is not obvious. Similarly, a paraconsistent theory might reject incomplete cases, and only recognize classical cases or complete but inconsistent cases.

For our purposes, we will take neither of those routes. Instead, we will briefly discuss a paraconsistent logical theory that *retains* our previous cases—both classical and incomplete but consistent cases—but further *expands* the range by acknowledging inconsistent cases (at least some of which are non-trivial). In this way, our paraconsistent theory is another broadening—from complete and consistent, to incomplete and consistent, to inconsistent.

6.3 Paraconsistent 'truth conditions'

The philosophical picture behind our paraconsistent theory has it that some sentences—some meaningful, declarative sentences—are both true and false. Such 'overdetermined sentences', according to a common metaphor, are *gluts*; they fall into the *intersection* of truth and falsity.

What are the truth conditions for our given connectives—the same basic connectives (plus defined connectives) from Chapters 4 and 5? A natural idea, which we will pursue, is as in Chapter 5: in effect, *retain the same truth conditions for molecular sentences*, with the only change occurring in the truth conditions for atomics.

6.3.1 *Atomics and Falsity*

Since we're retaining incomplete cases, we thereby retain the same 'breakdown' between falsity and untruth. (See Chapter 5.) As such, we will employ the same notation, using '$c \models_1 A$' to abbreviate '*A* is true-in-*c*', and '$c \models_0 A$' for '*A* is false-in-*c*'.

As in the previous chapters, we again won't give explicit truth conditions for atomic sentences. Instead, we simply stipulate the following *paraconsistent constraint*. What is important to see is that, as above, our aim is to retain the previous ideas—classical and paracomplete—but, now, merely broaden things to allow inconsistent cases. As such, our constraint looks a lot like our previous constraint on atomics (see Chapter 5), but it is slightly broader.

- *Paraconsistent Constraint for Atomics.* For any *atomic A* and any case *c*, exactly one of the following obtains.

  $c \models_1 A$ and $c \not\models_0 A$

  $c \not\models_1 A$ and $c \models_0 A$

  $c \not\models_1 A$ and $c \not\models_0 A$

  $c \models_1 A$ and $c \models_0 A$

For present purposes, we don't need to know *how* atomics get to be true-in-a-case or false-in-a-case; we just need to know that, for any case *c*, every atomic is either true-in-*c*, false-in-*c*, neither true-in-*c* nor false-in-*c*, or both true-in-*c* and false-in-*c*. (You should compare this constraint with the one from Chapter 5.)

Notice that, because we're retaining incomplete (and consistent) cases, our basic paraconsistent theory is also a paracomplete theory; it recognizes incomplete but consistent cases. On the other hand, this is not the same paracomplete theory as before, since we now recognize inconsistent cases. (You should think about this!)

6.3.2   *Molecular sentences*

With the paraconsistent constraint for atomics, we can give truth-in-a-case conditions for molecular sentences. There are various options one might pursue for such truth conditions. As in the basic paracomplete approach (Chapter 5), we have to give both truth conditions and falsity conditions; we must specify the conditions under which sentences are true-in-a-case, and conditions under which they're false-in-a-case.

As with the basic paracomplete approach, we stick as closely to the *classical* truth conditions (see Chapter 4) as possible.

Definition 35. (Basic Paraconsistent Truth and Falsity Conditions) *Where c is any (paraconsistent) case, and A and B any sentences of $\mathcal{L}$,[3] the paraconsistent conditions for the basic connectives are as follows.*

Conjunction: $c \models_1 A \wedge B$ if and only if $c \models_1 A$ and $c \models_1 B$.
Conjunction: $c \models_0 A \wedge B$ if and only if $c \models_0 A$ or $c \models_0 B$.

Disjunction: $c \models_1 A \vee B$ if and only if $c \models_1 A$ or $c \models_1 B$.
Disjunction: $c \models_0 A \vee B$ if and only if $c \models_0 A$ and $c \models_0 B$.

Negation: $c \models_1 \neg A$ if and only if $c \models_0 A$.
Negation: $c \models_0 \neg A$ if and only if $c \models_1 A$.[4]

Observe that the foregoing conditions are exactly our basic paracomplete conditions, which, as noted in Chapter 5, are (in effect) just the familiar classical conditions. The difference, of course, is that now some of our cases are inconsistent. That the given conditions are (in effect) the same as before shouldn't be surprising, since, as above, our paraconsistent theory simply *expands* the range of cases beyond our previous ones; it does not remove any of the previous cases.

As before, one can now see the basic paracomplete theory (from Chapter 5) as what you get from our basic paraconsistent theory if you ignore inconsistent cases. In turn, the basic classical theory is what you get from the paraconsistent theory if you ignore both the inconsistent and the incomplete cases. As such, the basic classical and the basic paracomplete theories may be seen as a narrow versions of our broader, basic paraconsistent (and paracomplete) theory—our basic 'glutty and gappy' theory. (Re-

---

[3] As in the previous chapter, $\mathcal{L}$ is a language with the basic connectives of conjunction, disjunction, and negation.

[4] Note: as in Chapter 5, given these conditions on Negation, the paraconsistent constraint on atomics yields the following for any paraconsistent case c.

$c \models_1 A$ and $c \not\models_1 \neg A$
$c \not\models_1 A$ and $c \models_1 \neg A$
$c \not\models_1 A$ and $c \not\models_1 \neg A$
$c \models_1 A$ and $c \models_1 \neg A$

call that we still allow 'gaps' in our basic paraconsistent theory; we now also allow 'gluts'.)

6.4   Paraconsistent consequence

As you know, B is a consequence of A iff there's no case in which A is true but B not true. In the present approach, cases are *paraconsistent cases*, which are *either* classical cases *or* incomplete but consistent cases *or* inconsistent cases. Given the truth (and falsity) conditions above, we can see a few notable features of our basic paraconsistent consequence relation.

6.4.1   *Paraconsistent and classical consequence*

For purposes of comparison, let us use '$\vdash_{bc}$', as before, for *basic classical consequence*, and use '$\vdash_{FDE}$' for our given *basic paraconsistent consequence* relation.[5] One notable fact about the relation between the two consequence relations—namely, the basic classical and basic paraconsistent relations—is the result that we previously had (Chapter 5).

CP2. Let $\mathcal{X}$ be any set of $\mathcal{L}$ sentences, and A any sentence of $\mathcal{L}$. Fact: if $\mathcal{X} \vdash_{FDE} A$ then $\mathcal{X} \vdash_{bc} A$.

The reason behind CP2 is just as with CP, from Chapter 5. Consequence is absence of counterexample, absence of any (relevant) case in which the premises are true but conclusion not true. Since the paraconsistent theory recognizes all classical cases, and keeps the same truth (and falsity) conditions, CP2 is straightforward: if there's no counterexample to the argument from $\mathcal{X}$ to A among all of the paraconsistent cases (including, of course, the classical cases), then there's no classical counterexample to the given argument. (You should compare this to the proof given for CP in Chapter 5.)

CP2 tells us something important about the relation between our basic classical consequence relation and our broader paraconsistent consequence relation: namely, that the latter is a *proper*

---

[5]'FDE' is the now-fairly-standard name of this particular paraconsistent (and, as we'll note below, paracomplete) logic; the name is for what Anderson and Belnap called a logic of first degree entailment (FDE), or the 'logic of tautological entailments'. See Anderson and Belnap 1975; Anderson, Belnap and Dunn 1992.

part of the former. In other words, the basic classical consequence relation is 'stronger' than our basic paracomplete one: the former has the latter as a proper part—a 'sub-relation'. CP2 tells us that any arguments that are valid according to the paraconsistent theory are valid according to the classical theory. As it turns out, the converse doesn't hold; there are some arguments that are valid according to the classical theory but not the paracomplete theory. (Can you think of one?) The reason is that the latter theory recognizes more cases than the classical theory, and hence recognizes more 'potential counterexamples'.

As with CP, from Chapter 5, CP2 tells us that, while our language may have both gappy and glutty sentences, it may also enjoy an entirely precise, classical fragment. Once again, for example, the mathematical or scientific fragment of our language might be perfectly precise and, in effect, classical, even though our broader language is 'indeterminate' in parts and 'overdeterminate' in parts.

6.4.2 *Absence of logical truths*

Since we still have all of our previous incomplete cases, we still have all of our previous counterexamples. Hence, there are no logical truths in our basic paraconsistent theory.[6]

6.5 Formal picture

As in Chapters 4 and 5, we are concentrating on a language with only a few basic connectives, and we are ignoring any structure within our atomic sentences. Our aim in this section is to briefly sketch a formal picture of our given paraconsistent logical theory of such a language. Towards that end, we will give a sketch of a formal language, a sketch of the 'semantics' (viz., truth conditions) for the language, and then define the consequence relation on the given language. What follows, as in Chapter 5, presupposes the set-theoretic tools that you learned in Chapter 3.

---

[6]See this chapter's exercises for a non-paracomplete variant of our basic paraconsistent theory.

6.5.1   *Syntax*

The syntax of our language $\mathcal{L}$ is exactly the same as in Chapters 4 and 5. The difference between the basic classical and basic paracomplete accounts of $\mathcal{L}$ arises at the level of semantics.

6.5.2   *Semantics*

As before, the key ingredients of logical consequence are *cases* and *truth-in-a-case* (and also *falsity-in-a-case*) conditions. Our concern, in this chapter, is with the basic paraconsistent theory. The question is: how shall we model our paraconsistent cases?

There are various ways of modeling our given cases. We will stick to an approach that is similar to the approach taken towards modeling our previous sorts of cases. As before, we will take our cases to be (modeled by) certain functions—ones obeying various constraints—from our set $\mathcal{S}$ of sentences into our set $\mathcal{V}$ of 'semantic values'. One *difference*, of course, is that we will *expand* our set of 'semantic values' from $\{1, n, 0\}$ to $\{1, b, n, 0\}$ (where b, now, may be thought to mark the semantic status of being *both true and false*). The idea, intuitively, is that the paraconsistent theory retains the previous semantic values; however, it also recognizes more options—namely, 'overdeterminacy' or 'gluts'. Intuitively, one can think of the value b as marking 'overdetermined' or 'glutty' sentences, the idea being that if A is assigned b in a case, then, intuitively, it is 'overdetermined' or 'glutty' in that case.

To be clearer, our semantics begins with a set of semantic values, namely, $\mathcal{V} = \{1, b, n, 0\}$. What's different from our previous accounts is that we now need to be explicit about our set $\mathcal{D}$ of so-called *designated values*. Intuitively, the designated values can be thought of as different 'ways of being true'. In our previous logical theories, no sentence could be both true and false; they were only true, if true at all. In our current, paraconsistent theory, some sentences can be only true, as before, but they can also be true *and* false. As such, we have expanded our semantic values, and we now designate both 1 and b. It is the designated values in terms of which we define *truth in a case* (and, as below, consequence). Our set $\mathcal{D}$ of designated values is $\{1, b\}$.

With $\mathcal{V}$ so given, and designated values so specified, we let our *cases* be functions v from $\mathcal{S}$ into $\mathcal{V}$, so that we have $v(A) = 1$ or $v(A) = \mathsf{b}$ or $v(A) = \mathsf{n}$ or $v(A) = 0$, for every sentence A and any such case v.

We define *truth in a case* as follows: A is *true-in-a-case* v (remember that our 'cases' are now functions) if and only if $v(A) \in \mathcal{D}$, that is, $v(A) = 1$ or $v(A) = \mathsf{b}$.

What about *falsity in a case*? As before, we certainly want that A is false-in-a-case v if $v(A) = 0$. But notice that we are now also considering the idea that A may be true *and* false. Any sentence that is true and false is false. So, any glut, while true, is also false. Accordingly, since b is representing our 'glutty' category, we also say that A is false in case v if $v(A) = \mathsf{b}$. Our definition of *falsity in a case*, then, is as follows: A is *false-in-a-case* v iff $v(A) = 0$ or $v(A) = \mathsf{b}$.

As with our previous 'formal models', we do *not* want to allow just *any* old function from $\mathcal{S}$ into $\mathcal{V}$ to count as a paraconsistent case! After all, there are certainly functions from $\mathcal{S}$ into $\mathcal{V}$ that do not respect the paraconsistent truth conditions. Consider, for example, a function v such that $v(A \vee \neg A) = 0$. This is certainly a function from $\mathcal{S}$ into $\mathcal{V}$, but it doesn't respect the given truth conditions for disjunction and negation.

Following our usual approach (see previous chapters), we rule out such 'unwanted' functions from our set of cases by invoking the following truth conditions. In particular, we say that a function v, from $\mathcal{S}$ into $\mathcal{V}$, is a *paraconsistent case* if and only if it 'obeys' the following truth conditions.

$\neg$		$\wedge$	1	b	n	0		$\vee$	1	b	n	0
0	1	1	1	1	b	n	0		1	1	1	1	1
b	b	b	b	b	b	0	0		b	1	b	1	b
n	n	n	n	n	0	n	0		n	1	1	n	n
1	0	0	0	0	0	0	0		0	1	b	n	0

These tables look more complicated than the previous ones, but that's only because there are more values to look at. On inspection, you'll see that, if you remove the glut value b, the tables are exactly our previous, basic paracomplete tables.

As before, the given truth conditions are fairly classical. For example, a negation $\neg A$ is true-in-a-case iff its negatum is false-in-the-given-case; and $\neg A$ is false-in-a-given-case iff its negatum is true-in-the-given-case. What one has to remember, of course, is that we're now considering sentences that can be true and false, that is, sentences that are true but also have true negations. This is why, for example, $v(A) = \mathsf{b}$ iff $v(\neg A) = \mathsf{b}$. The idea, as above, is that if A is true and false, then its negation is also true and false. And this is represented in the given truth conditions.

Similarly, a conjunction is true-in-a-case iff both conjuncts are true in the case; and it is false-in-a-case iff at least one conjunct is false-in-the-case. The difference, again, is that we now have gluts, but the conditions remain classical in spirit. For example, if A is true and false, and B is just true, then $A \wedge B$ is true (since both conjuncts are true) but it is also false (since at least one conjunct, namely A, is false), and hence $\neg(A \wedge B)$ is true and false. (If you do not see this, you should think about it in relation to the above tables.) The same 'classical' spirit holds also for disjunction.

The final step, in giving the semantics, is to specify our target relation: namely, logical consequence. The definition, as usual, is just an instance of our recipe in Chapter 1. To make things simpler, we will explicitly invoke our designated values $\mathcal{D} = \{1, \mathsf{b}\}$.

Definition 36. (Basic Paraconsistent Consequence) *B is a logical consequence of A if and only if there is no paraconsistent case v such that $v(A) \in \mathcal{D}$ but $v(B) \notin \mathcal{D}$. (In other words, there's no case v in which A is true but B not true.)*

Generalizing, we say that *v satisfies* a sentence A iff $v(A) \in \mathcal{D}$ (i.e., iff A is true-in-the-given-case). In turn, where $\mathcal{X}$ is any set of $\mathcal{L}$ sentences, we say that *v satisfies $\mathcal{X}$* iff v satisfies every member of $\mathcal{X}$. With this terminology, we give our more general definition of basic paraconsistent consequence as follows.

Definition 37. (General Basic Paraconsistent Consequence) *$\mathcal{X} \vdash A$ if and only if there is no paraconsistent case v that satisfies $\mathcal{X}$ but not A.*

« *Parenthetical remark.* If disambiguation is required, we will use '$\vdash_{FDE}$' for the basic paraconsistent relation defined via paraconsistent cases. *End parenthetical.* »

You should think about this definition, compare it with the 'general recipe' of logical consequence and the classical account, and also evaluate various argument forms for (basic paraconsistent) validity. Note that a paraconsistent *counterexample* need not be a case in which the conclusion is *false*; it need only be a case in which the conclusion is not designated—that is, either n or 0.

6.6 Defined connectives

We will use the same defined connectives as before: '$A \to B$' is shorthand for $\neg A \vee B$, and similarly '$A \leftrightarrow B$' is shorthand for $(A \to B) \wedge (B \to A)$. As in Chapter 5, the truth conditions for these defined connectives are simply the resulting truth conditions for the corresponding sentences that use only our Basic (primitive) connectives—for example, the truth conditions for $\neg A \vee B$ and $(\neg A \vee B) \wedge (\neg B \vee A)$. In our given paraconsistent setting, the given conditions are represented in the following tables.

$\to$	1	b	n	0
1	1	b	n	0
b	1	b	1	b
n	1	1	n	n
0	1	1	1	1

$\leftrightarrow$	1	b	n	0
1	1	b	n	0
b	b	b	1	b
n	n	1	n	n
0	0	b	n	1

6.7 Some notable forms

Logical theories of a language provide an account of the (logical) behavior of the language's connectives. Such behavior is manifest is in the consequence relation, in particular, the valid argument forms involving those connectives.

Our current, paraconsistent consequence relation, as noted, is a 'sub-relation' of the basic classical consequence relation. Moreover, because we've retained all of our incomplete cases and the same truth- and falsity-in-a-case conditions, there are no logical truths according to our basic paraconsistent (and paracomplete) theory (viz., FDE). By way of comparing our current theory with the previous two, consider the following items.

- Excluded Middle: $\nvdash_{FDE} A \vee \neg A$
- Non-Contradiction: $\nvdash_{FDE} \neg(A \wedge \neg A)$
- Modus Ponens: $A \to B, A \nvdash_{FDE} B$
- Modus Tollens: $A \to B, \neg B \nvdash_{FDE} \neg A$
- Disjunctive Syllogism: $A \vee B, \neg A \nvdash_{FDE} B$
- Contraposition: $A \to B \dashv\vdash_{FDE} \neg B \to \neg A$

- Explosion: $A, \neg A \nvdash_{FDE} B$
- Addition: $A \vdash_{FDE} A \vee B$
- Adjunction: $A, B \vdash_{FDE} A \wedge B$
- Simplification: $A \wedge B \vdash_{FDE} A$
- De Morgan: $\neg(A \vee B) \dashv\vdash_{FDE} \neg A \wedge \neg B$
- De Morgan: $\neg(A \wedge B) \dashv\vdash_{FDE} \neg A \vee \neg B$
- Double Negation: $\neg\neg A \dashv\vdash_{FDE} A$

Notice that, in virtue of admitting our inconsistent cases, we have significantly weakened the logic, that is, that many of the previously valid arguments are now invalid. This is not terribly surprising, since we have broadened our range of potential counterexamples.

You should provide counterexamples to the given invalid argument forms, and prove that the given valid forms are valid (according to the paraconsistent theory). For now, it is worth noticing an important invalidity, namely, Explosion.

We said, above, that there seem to be sentences of our language that are true and false—peculiar sentences, like the starred sentence or ticked sentence.[7] On the other hand, surely not *all* sentences of our language are true and false. If Explosion were valid (i.e., if the form $A, \neg A \therefore B$ were valid), then any glut would *explode* the language: *all* sentences would be true and false! Fortunately, Explosion doesn't hold, at least according to paraconsistent theories.

That Explosion is not valid according to our basic paraconsistent theory may be seen via the following counterexample. Let $v(A) = $ b and $v(B) = 0$. (You could also let $v(B) = $ n, which would provide a different counterexample with the same effect.) Given the truth conditions for negation, we have it that $v(\neg A) = $ b since $v(A) = $ b. But, then, both premises are true (i.e., designated) in the given case, but the conclusion is not true (i.e., not designated) in the given case. This is a counterexample to Explosion.

Similarly, it might be useful to see a counterexample for Modus Ponens. Let $v(A) = $ b and $v(B) = 0$. (Again, you could instead let

---

[7]Of course, you might disagree that there are any such gluts in our language. For present purposes, the aim is only to explore the basic idea!

$v(B) = $ n, which, unlike where $v(B) = 0$, yields $v(A \to B) = 1$ where $v(A) = $ b.) Given the truth conditions for negation, we have it that $v(\neg A) = $ b since $v(A) = $ b. In turn, given the truth conditions for our conditional, we have it that $v(A \to B) = $ b. But, now, notice that both of our premises are true in the given case—that is, both sentences have a designated value. Hence, we have a case in which our premises are all true (designated) but the conclusion isn't. This is a counterexample to the given argument form, namely, Modus Ponens.

6.8 Summary and looking ahead

Summary. Motivated by apparent 'overdeterminacy', our basic paraconsistent theory of logical consequence broadens our previous range of cases. In particular, we retain all of our previous cases but we add another type, namely, inconsistent cases—be they incomplete or complete. The resulting consequence relation is weaker than our previous relations, but classical logic can still be seen as a special case of our broad, paraconsistent framework—namely, it's the logic you get if you ignore inconsistent and incomplete cases. One significant feature of our given paraconsistent theory is the failure of Explosion. Intuitively, we should expect Explosion to fail, at least if our language has some overdeterminacy but is not entirely overdetermined.

Looking Ahead. In the next chapter, we keep our stock of connectives the same, but we delve deeper into our atomics. Instead of treating our atomic sentences as having no significant logical parts, we 'break them open' (as it were) to find a few logically significant bits.

Further Reading. Any of the Beall & van Frassen, Priest, and Restall textbooks mentioned in previous chapters (under 'further reading') provide useful further reading for our given paraconsistent logical theory. (Priest's given textbook also provides a fairly wide discussion of many different approaches to paraconsistent logical theory.) One of the pioneering cases for gluts is Priest 2006, and a more recent discussion is Beall 2009.

Exercises

1. Given your understanding of *designated values*, answer the following questions. What are the designated values of our basic classical theory (see Chapter 4)? What are the designated values of our basic paracomplete theory (see Chapter 5)?

2. One might, as mentioned in the text, have reason to reject indeterminacy but, in light of the Liar (or the like), nonetheless acknowledge overdeterminacy. A logical theory along these lines was first advanced by Asenjo (1966) but known widely from Graham Priest's work (1979) as LP for 'logic of paradox'. The difference between LP and our basic paraconsistent theory is that the former ignores incomplete cases. In particular, everything is the same except that $\mathcal{V} = \{1, b, 0\}$, but $\mathcal{D}$ (the designated values) remains $\{1, b\}$, as we have it. Question: are there any logical truths in LP? If so, prove it. If not, explain why not.

3. Are there any cases in which $A \wedge \neg A$ is true (designated), according to our basic paraconsistent theory? If so, give an example. If not, say why not.

4. Are there any cases in which $\neg(A \wedge \neg A)$ is not true (not designated), according to our basic paraconsistent theory? If so, give an example. If not, say why not.

5. For each of the valid forms in §6.7, give a proof that they're valid. For each of the invalid forms, give a counterexample.

6. Explain why the following claim is true: if $\mathcal{X} \vdash_{FDE} A$ then $\mathcal{X} \vdash_{K3} A$.

7. Are the following argument forms valid in our basic paraconsistent (and paracomplete) theory (viz., FDE)? Provide a proof (of validity) or counterexample (for invalidity) in each case. Also, note whether or not the given forms are valid in the basic paracomplete (viz., K3) or basic classical theories (see previous chapters).

   (a) $A \to B, \neg A \to B \therefore B$
   (b) $(A \vee B) \wedge C, A \to \neg C \therefore B$
   (c) $A \to B, B \to C \therefore A \to C$

Sample answers

Answer 6. The key point to see is that the FDE and K3 (i.e., our basic glutty–gappy and basic gappy) theories agree on the truth conditions for all connectives; it's just that the former theory acknowledges more 'semantic options' (notably, gluts) than the latter acknowledges. Close observation shows that, if you ignore the gluts (e.g., the value b) in the FDE (basic glutty–gappy) theory, you simply wind up with K3 (i.e., our basic gappy-but-no-gluts theory)! In other words, FDE and K3 agree on all cases that don't involve gluts: whatever the one counts as a counterexample, the other counts as a counterexample (provided that, as above, we're ignoring gluts). In yet other words: any case that K3 counts as a case (and, hence, as a potential counterexample) is one that FDE counts as a case (and, hence, as a potential counterexample). Hence, the K3 cases are a subset of the FDE cases. And that's the key insight: if there's no FDE counterexample to an argument, then there's no K3 counterexample to the argument. Hence, if $\mathcal{X} \vdash_{FDE} A$ (i.e., there's no basic glutty–gappy counterexample to an argument), then $\mathcal{X} \vdash_{K3} A$ (i.e., there's no basic gappy counterexample to the argument).

PART III

INNARDS, IDENTITY, AND QUANTIFIERS

7

Atomic Innards

> *Humor can be dissected as a frog can,*
> *but the thing dies in the process*
> *and the innards are discouraging*
> *to any but the pure scientific mind.*
> *– E. B. White*

So far, we have kept our basic stock of connectives the same, but expanded our stock of 'cases'. We have so far ignored any possible structure within our *atomic sentences*. As a result, there was nothing much to say about how an atomic comes to be true (or whathaveyou) in a given case. Instead, we merely said that each atomic gets exactly one of the given semantic values (true, false, whathaveyou). In this chapter we change things. We look 'inside' of atomics, bringing out a little bit of structure. In turn, we will say a little bit about how atomics come to be true, false or whathaveyou in a given case.

7.1 Atomic innards: names and predicates

Originally, the term 'atom' meant *indivisible*. If you found an atom, you found a basic, indivisible item. In chemistry and physics, where one searches for the basic physical atoms, the term 'atom' was initially applied to molecules—though they were thought to be atoms (i.e., fundamental, indivisible, etc.). As it turned out, such chemical 'atoms' could be divided; they were built out of even more basic parts—what we now call *atoms*.[1]

As in Chapter 2, our language has its own sort of atoms and molecules, namely, atomic and molecular sentences. For our purposes, atomics have no (logical) connectives in them. As such, and because we have been interested in the basic connectives, we

---

[1] As it turned out, even these 'atoms' were further divisible; we now have 'sub-atomic' parts (quarks, etc.).

have treated our atomics as structureless items. (In our formal language, we have let our atoms be structureless, lowercase letters, '*p*', '*q*', etc.) Just as in chemistry, it turns out that, in logic, it's useful to acknowledge some structure 'inside' of our atomics. This is not to say that atomics now contain *connectives*; they don't. The point is that, for purposes of a richer logical theory, we need to acknowledge various kinds of parts that make up atomics.

Fortunately, the relevant 'atomic innards' are familiar items. In particular, we will (for now) recognize two different types of expressions that make up atomic sentences: namely, predicates and names.[2] Consider, for example, basic atomic sentences like the following.

1. Max is happy.

2. Max is bigger than Agnes.

3. Agnes is happier than Max.

4. Katrina is between Max and Agnes.

Each of the above sentences is made up of a predicate and one or more names. For example, (1) is made up of the *unary* predicate 'is happy' and the name 'Max'. (2) is made up of the *binary* predicate '. . . is bigger than . . . ' and the names 'Max' and 'Agnes'. Sentence (3) is similar to (2), as it has a binary predicate and two names. Sentence (4) is made up of the *ternary* predicate '. . . is between . . . and . . . ' and the names 'Katrina', 'Max', and 'Agnes'.

From a semantic perspective, *names*, of course, function to pick out objects, while *predicates* function to express 'properties' or relations—features or characteristics. From a *syntactic* perspective, we will understand *n*-ary predicates as follows.

Definition 38. (*n*-ary Predicate) *An n-ary predicate (qua syntactic item) takes n many names (or, more broadly, singular terms) to make a sentence.*

---

[2]Atomic innards are expanded a bit in subsequent chapters. Due to space, however, we do not consider other philosophically important sorts of singular terms (e.g., definite descriptions like 'the first person to know that 1+1=2'), but this book (particularly subsequent chapters) gives you sufficient competence to jump into such areas—e.g., Russell's theory of definite descriptions (which is mentioned in just about every book on the philosophy of language or philosophy of logic).

Just as an n-ary connective, syntactically conceived, takes n many sentences to make a sentence, an n-ary *predicate* takes n many *names* to make a sentence.

What, then, do the innards of our atomics look like? The answer, in short, is that atomics are made up of an n-ary predicate and n many names. That's basically it, except for a qualification about order. In particular, the *order* in which names occur in an atomic matters. For example, consider the binary predicate 'loves' and the names 'Max' and 'Agnes'. Our predicate, being binary, requires two names to make a sentence. The point of order is that 'Max loves Agnes' and 'Agnes loves Max' are different atomic sentences; they use the same names and the same predicate, but the *order* of names is different, and so the resulting (atomic) sentence is different.

7.2 Truth and falsity conditions for atomics

What do names do? As above, they serve to pick out objects. *How* names pick out objects is an ongoing philosophical issue; however, we will ignore the issue and just assume that, at least in general, names pick out objects. Let us say that the object picked out by a name is the *denotation* of the name. In general, if x is the denotation of a name α,[3] we say that α *denotes* x. For example, 'Max' denotes Max, your name denotes you, and 'Benjamin Franklin' denotes the inventor of bifocals.

What about predicates? There are various answers that one might give to this question. For our purposes, we will assume that predicates are used to classify objects. In particular, predicates can be true or false of objects. For example, 'is a cat' is true of Max, but it is false of Katrina. Similarly, 'is a human' is true of Katrina but false of Max. In this way, we classify Max as *being a cat*, and Katrina as *being a non-cat*, and similarly classify Katrina as *being a human* and Max as *being non-human*. (Of course, more informative classifications are also available.)

Let us say that a predicate's *extension* is the set of things of which the predicate is true, and a predicate's *antiextension* is the

---

[3]Here, 'α' (pronounced *alpha*), which is the first (lowercase) letter of the Greek alphabet, is a so-called metavariable ranging over names; you can just think of α (or, in places, α_i) as a name.

set of things of which a predicate is false. So, for example, Max is in the extension of 'is a cat' while Katrina is in the antiextension of 'is a cat'. Similarly, Katrina is in the extension of 'is a human' while Max is in the antiextension of 'is a human'.

Definition 39. (Extension) *The extension of a predicate is the set of things of which the predicate is true.*

Definition 40. (Antiextension) *The antiextension of a predicate is the set of things of which the predicate is false.*

With this terminology, we can give truth and falsity conditions of atomics as follows. Concentrate, first, on atomics that involve only a *unary* predicate Π.[4]

- An atomic sentence $\Pi\alpha$ is true iff the denotation of α is in the extension of Π.

- An atomic sentence $\Pi\alpha$ is false iff the denotation of α is in the antiextension of Π.

This account only covers unary predicates. If, as suggested in Chapter 3, we equate an ordered 1-tuple $\langle x \rangle$ with x itself, then we can give general truth and falsity conditions for all atomics (as opposed to those that use only a unary predicate). Here, we let Π be any n-ary predicate (e.g., unary, binary, etc), and let $\alpha_1, \ldots, \alpha_n$ be n many names, and we let $a_1, \ldots, a_n$ be n many objects. In turn, let object a_i be the denotation of name α_i, for each i (e.g., α_2 denotes a_2, etc.).

- An atomic $\Pi\alpha_1, \ldots, \alpha_n$ is true iff $\langle a_1, \ldots, a_n \rangle$ is in the extension of Π.

- An atomic $\Pi\alpha_1, \ldots, \alpha_n$ is false iff $\langle a_1, \ldots, a_n \rangle$ is in the antiextension of Π.

So, for example, 'Max loves Agnes' is true iff $\langle$Max, Agnes$\rangle$ is in the extension of 'loves'. In turn, sentence (4) from §7.1 is true iff $\langle$Katrina, Max, Agnes$\rangle$ is in the extension of '... is between ... and ...'. And so on.

---

[4]I used the Greek (uppercase) letter 'Π' (viz., Pi) for a so-called metavariable for arbitrary predicates (usually of our formal language). If you want, just think of 'Π' as standing for any predicate (well, in the current case, *unary* predicate).

We can make this a bit more transparent, and perhaps slightly more general, if we introduce a bit more notation. In particular, let $\delta(\alpha)$ be the denotation of the name α.[5] Here, we are supposing that δ is a function that serves to give our names their respective denotations. With this in mind, we can put the above truth and falsity conditions as follows.

- $\Pi\alpha_1, \ldots, \alpha_n$ is true iff $\langle \delta(\alpha_1), \ldots, \delta(\alpha_n) \rangle$ is in the extension of Π.
- $\Pi\alpha_1, \ldots, \alpha_n$ is false iff $\langle \delta(\alpha_1), \ldots, \delta(\alpha_n) \rangle$ is in the antiextension of Π.

Of course, we are chiefly interested in *truth-in-a-case* and *falsity-in-a-case* conditions, but a minor modification of the above gives us what we want.

- $\Pi\alpha_1, \ldots, \alpha_n$ is true-in-a-case c iff *in case* c, $\langle \delta(\alpha_1), \ldots, \delta(\alpha_n) \rangle$ is in the extension of Π.
- $\Pi\alpha_1, \ldots, \alpha_n$ is false-in-a-case c iff *in case* c, $\langle \delta(\alpha_1), \ldots, \delta(\alpha_n) \rangle$ is in the antiextension of Π.

Putting things this way raises the obvious question: what, now, are these cases? What, for example, do we mean by *in case* c *such and so is in the (anti) extension of a predicate*?

7.3   Cases, domains, and interpretation functions

Recall that, for our purposes, 'cases' are things in which sentences may be true or false. Until now, we didn't need to say much more about such cases, except just that: viz., that sentences are true-in-them or false-in-them (or neither true- nor false-, or perhaps both). Until now, there was little need to talk about *how* sentences came to be true- or false-in-cases.

Things are now different. While we haven't said *how* a name comes to denote an object, or *how* a predicate gets an extension or antiextension, we have nonetheless said something about how atomics come to be true- (or false-) in-a-case. In particular, truth in a case (similarly falsity in a case) turns on denotations of terms and the extension (or antiextension) of predicates. What this suggests, then, is that our cases—whatever else they may be—come

---

[5]The letter 'δ' (pronounced *delta*) is the fourth (lowercase) letter of the Greek alphabet; we are letting δ be our denotation function.

equipped with denotations of terms, as well as extensions and antiextensions of predicates. The idea, in short, is that our cases come equipped with their own 'story' (as it were) about what our names denote (in that case) and what the extensions (and antiextensions) of our predicates are (in that case). Moreover, our cases have their own 'story' about *what objects exist.*

The matter might be thought of as follows. Our cases come equipped with a set D of objects, where D is the *domain* of the given case. For example, one case c might be such that $D = \{\text{Max}, \text{Agnes}\}$, while another case c' might have a different domain, say $\{1, 2, 3, \text{Katrina}, \text{Max}\}$. The domain of any given case is the set of objects that exist in that case.

Similarly, cases have their own say on the denotations of terms. As above, each case c comes equipped with a domain D, which comprises the objects that may serve as denotations in the given case. In addition to having a domain, we can also think of each case c as having a *denotation function* δ, a function from the names in our language into c's domain D. Even if, for example, two cases, say c and c', have the same domain, they may disagree on the denotations of terms. In case c, we might have it that $\delta(\alpha)$ is (say) Max, while in case c' we might have it that $\delta(\alpha)$ is (say) Agnes. In that respect, one can think of the two cases as giving different denotations to the same name α.

Finally, our cases also have their own say on the extensions and antiextensions of predicates. In one case, the extension of Π might be (say) $\{1, 2, 3\}$, while the extension of Π in another case might be different. Of course, the extensions (similarly, antiextensions) will always be sets of (n-tuples of) objects from the given domain. The point, though, is that even when two cases agree on the same domain (i.e., they have the same domain), they might disagree on the extensions and antiextensions of predicates; they might disagree on which of our predicates are true or false of the given objects; they might disagree, as it were, on how the given objects are to be 'classified'.

Putting all of this together, our *cases*—whatever else they may be—provide the following. Where c is any case, we have

- the domain of c, namely, D, which comprises all objects that exist in (or according to) case c.

- denotation: to each name α in the language, the case c provides a denotation of α, namely, $\delta(\alpha)$, which is an element of D (c's domain).

- extensions and antiextensions: to each n-ary predicate Π in the language, the case c provides an extension and antiextension of Π, namely, a set of n-tuples 'made up of' elements of D.

7.4   Classical, paracomplete and paraconsistent

We've talked broadly about cases. How, if at all, do our given logical theories differ in their accounts of such cases? All agree, of course, that cases must provide the basic resources required for atomics to be true-in-a-case or false-in-a-case (e.g., domain of objects, denotations of terms, extensions and antiextensions of predicates). The question concerns how, if at all, our given theories differ in what such cases are like.

The answer is that each theory places different constraints on what goes on inside of cases—in particular, on what happens with extensions and antiextensions. Let us introduce two constraints on extensions and antiextensions. For convenience, let $\mathcal{E}^+$ and $\mathcal{E}^-$ be the extension and antiextension of some arbitrary predicate.

- *Exhaustion.* $\mathcal{E}^+ \cup \mathcal{E}^- = D$. In other words, for any case c, any predicate Π, and any object x in c's domain, x is either in the extension of Π or in the antiextension of Π (i.e., Π is either true of x or Π is false of x in the given case).

- *Exclusion.* $\mathcal{E}^+ \cap \mathcal{E}^- = \emptyset$. In other words, for any case c, any predicate Π, and any object x in c's domain, x is not in the extension of Π *and* the antiextension of Π (i.e., Π isn't true *and* false of x in the given case).

Consider the classical theory. According to it, every sentence—and, hence, every atomic—is either true-in-c or false-in-c (but not both). Accordingly, the classical theory imposes both the Exhaustion and Exclusion constraints on cases. In turn, a paracomplete theory drops the Exhaustion constraint. In turn, a paraconsistent theory drops the Exclusion constraint.

7.5   A formal picture

This will be very brief. As above, our cases are more involved. For present purposes, we will present a formal picture of the basic paraconsistent (and paracomplete) theory, but one that now takes account of our new atomic sentences.

7.5.1 *Syntax*

This is the same as before, except we now add a few things.

- A set of predicates: $F, G, H, \ldots, S, T$ with or without numerical subscripts.

- A set of names: a, b, c, d with or without numerical subscripts.

These sets expand our 'vocabulary' or 'building blocks'. We must now expand our definition of *sentences*.

1. Atomics: if Π is an n-ary predicate, and $\alpha_1, \ldots, \alpha_n$ are n many names, then $\Pi\alpha_1, \ldots, \alpha_n$ is an atomic sentence.
2. All atomics are sentences.
3. If A and B are sentences, so too are $\neg A, (A \wedge B)$, and $(A \vee B)$.
4. Nothing but what's from (1)–(3) is a sentence.[6]

We now move to semantics.

7.5.2 *Semantics*

What are our cases? We now take (or model) cases to be structures $\langle D, \delta \rangle$. So, a given case c is now some such structure $\langle D, \delta \rangle$ where D is the domain of c, and δ is a function. The job of δ, in any such case, is to provide denotations to all names, and extensions and antiextensions to all predicates. In particular, for any given case $\langle D, \delta \rangle$, the function δ (in the given case) does the following two jobs.

1. Denotation: δ provides denotations to all names; so, $\delta(\alpha)$ is an object in D, for every name α.
2. Predication: for any n-ary predicate Π, the function δ assigns an extension to Π and an antiextension to Π.[7] In effect, you can think of $\delta(\Pi)$ as a pair $\langle \mathcal{E}_\Pi^+, \mathcal{E}_\Pi^- \rangle$, where $\mathcal{E}_\Pi^+$ is the extension of Π and $\mathcal{E}_\Pi^-$ the antiextension, according to c (i.e., according to c's denotation function δ).[8]

---

[6]Since we're treating $\rightarrow$ and $\leftrightarrow$ as defined connectives, we have these sorts of *defined sentences*—e.g., $(A \rightarrow B)$, which is covered as $(\neg A \vee B)$.

[7]So, $\delta(\Pi) \subseteq D^n \times D^n$ for any n-ary predicate Π.

[8]Notation: if no confusion is likely to arise, we sometimes write 'Π^+' for the extension of Π, namely, $\mathcal{E}_\Pi^+$, and similarly for the antiextension Π^- of Π.

Given our cases, we now give truth-in-a-case and falsity-in-a-case conditions. To do this, we resort to our familiar notation from previous chapters, where '$c \models_1 A$' abbreviates 'A is true-in-case-c' and '$c \models_0 A$' abbreviates 'A is false-in-case-c'. Moreover, we'll also use our notation from above for extension and antiextension.

- Atomics
  $$c \models_1 \Pi\alpha_1, \ldots, \alpha_n \text{ iff } \langle \delta(\alpha_1), \ldots, \delta(\alpha_n) \rangle \in \mathcal{E}_\Pi^+.$$
  $$c \models_0 \Pi\alpha_1, \ldots, \alpha_n \text{ iff } \langle \delta(\alpha_1), \ldots, \delta(\alpha_n) \rangle \in \mathcal{E}_\Pi^-.$$
- Negations
  $$c \models_1 \neg A \text{ iff } c \models_0 A.$$
  $$c \models_0 \neg A \text{ iff } c \models_1 A.$$
- Conjunctions
  $$c \models_1 A \wedge B \text{ iff } c \models_1 A \text{ and } c \models_1 B.$$
  $$c \models_0 A \wedge B \text{ iff } c \models_0 A \text{ or } c \models_0 B.$$
- Disjunctions
  $$c \models_1 A \vee B \text{ iff } c \models_1 A \text{ or } c \models_1 B.$$
  $$c \models_0 A \vee B \text{ iff } c \models_0 A \text{ and } c \models_0 B.$$

With the above truth and falsity conditions, we can now define consequence as usual, using the recipe from Chapter 1. To make things general, we say that case c *satisfies* sentence A iff $c \models_1 A$. In turn, where $\mathcal{X}$ is a set of sentences, we say that c satisfies $\mathcal{X}$ iff c satisfies every sentence in $\mathcal{X}$. Given this terminology, we define— in effect, our basic paraconsistent account of—consequence (viz., FDE) as follows.

- $\mathcal{X} \vdash A$ iff any case that satisfies $\mathcal{X}$ satisfies A.

7.6 Summary and looking ahead

Summary. We have introduced 'atomic innards', which are predicates and names. We have given truth and falsity conditions for such atomics. Because our truth-in-a-case and falsity-in-a-case conditions require more of cases, we have expanded our idea of cases. In effect, cases now come equipped with a domain of objects (viz., all that exists in the given case), a denotation function that assigns objects (from the domain) to all names in our language, and a function that assigns extensions and antiextensions to each predicate. To get the classical logical theory, one puts the Exhaustion and Exclusion constraints on cases (in particular, on extensions and antiextensions of all predicates). To get the para-complete (but non-paraconsistent) theory, one drops Exhaustion but retains Exclusion. To enjoy our broad, paraconsistent (and paracomplete) theory, one drops both Exclusion and Exhaustion.

Looking Ahead. In the next chapter, we introduce no new logical connectives, but we do introduce new logically significant bits: we expand our stock of 'logical expressions' by adding a new, *logical predicate*—namely, Identity.

Further Reading. Any standard textbook that covers so-called classical first-order logic will be a useful supplement to this chapter's topic(s); however, for the full non-classical account sketched here (wherein antiextensions become essential), a good source for further reading is Priest's textbook mentioned in previous chapters, namely, Priest 2008.

Exercises

1. Consider a case $c = \langle D, v \rangle$ where $D = \{1, 2, 3\}$, and $\delta(a) = 1$, $\delta(b) = 2$, and $\delta(d) = 3$, and $F^+ = \{1, 2\}$ and $F^- = \{1\}$. For each of the following, say whether it is true or false. If true, say why. If false, say why.

   (a) $c \models_1 Fa$
   (b) $c \models_0 Fa$
   (c) $c \models_1 \neg Fa$
   (d) $c \models_1 Fb \vee Fd$
   (e) $c \models_1 Fb \wedge Fd$
   (f) $c \models_1 \neg(Fb \vee Fd)$
   (g) $c \models_1 Fd \rightarrow Fb$

2. Construct a case in which $Fa \wedge \neg Fb$ is true.[9]

3. Construct a case in which $Fa \wedge \neg Fa$ is true.

4. Construct a case in which $Fa \vee \neg Fa$ is neither true nor false.

5. Notice that, without imposing further constraints, a case c might let $\emptyset$ be both the extension and antiextension of any (or all!) predicate(s) Π. What does this tell you about logical truths—sentences true-in-*all cases*?

---

[9]To construct a case, you have to specify the domain, the denotations of the various names, and the extensions and antiextensions of given predicates.

Sample answers

Answer 1c. $c \models_1 \neg Fa$ iff $c \models_0 Fa$ iff $\delta(a) \in F^-$. Since our given case c is such that $\delta(a) \in F^-$ (since $\delta(a)$ is 1, which is in the antiextension of F in our given case), we conclude that $c \models_1 \neg Fa$.

Answer 2. A case in which $Fa \wedge \neg Fb$ is true as follows. Let $c = \langle D, \delta \rangle$, where $D = \{1, 2\}$ and $\delta(a) = 1$, $\delta(b) = 2$, and $F^+ = \{1\}$ and $F^- = \{2\}$. (NB: there are many other cases in which $Fa \wedge \neg Fb$ is true.)

8

Identity

I am that I am.
– God
Exodus 3:14

In the last chapter, we recognized 'atomic innards' by adding a set of predicates and names. In turn, we expanded our cases to cover predicates and names. Unlike the last chapter, this chapter adds a new *logical expression* (viz., an identity predicate), and in turn offers truth (and falsity) conditions for the new expression. (This is done by imposing constraints on our cases.)

8.1 Logical expressions and logical form

In Chapter 2, we noted that logicians tend to think of validity as a matter of logical form. So far, we have treated logical form as a matter of logical connectives: we specify different logical forms of sentences in terms of the logical connectives in our language. Moreover, we have so far recognized only (let us say) 'basic forms', forms defined out of (what we have called) basic connectives: *conjunctions, disjunctions,* and *negations.*[1] All of these basic connectives are sentential connectives: syntactically, they take sentences and make new sentences.

The notion of logical form need not be tied to sentential connectives. In general, the logical form of a sentence (and, in turn, that of arguments built from sentences) is defined via the *logical*

---

[1] These connectives are sometimes called *Boolean connectives* as a tribute to George Boole's logical work on them. We have avoided this terminology because it is sometimes used to mean *the classical theory of such (basic) connectives,* and we've looked at non-classical theories of such (basic) connectives. To avoid confusion, we simply cal them 'basic'. ('Sentential' or 'propositional' can also be used.)

expressions of the language. As above, we have so far acknowledged only sentential connectives as our logical expressions. Predicates, which we now have in the language, can also be logical expressions.

8.2 Validity involving identity

The chief aim of logic, as discussed in Chapter 1, is to specify what follows from what. None of the logical theories canvassed so far has the resources to count the following argument as valid.

1. Max is big.
2. Max is identical to Boydy.
3. Therefore, Boydy is big.

The only logical expressions that we (or our logical theories) have acknowledged so far are basic sentential connectives. But since the argument above is devoid of such connectives, its logical form amounts to nothing more than $A, B \therefore C$. And this form is invalid on all of our canvassed basic theories.

You might object that, since we now have predicates and names, there is more to the structure of the sentences than is revealed in form $A, B \therefore C$. After all, you might say, 'Max' and 'Boydy' are names, and 'is big' is a unary predicate; and 'is identical to' is a binary predicate. With all of this in hand, you might note (correctly) that a more discriminating form than the simple A-B-C form is as follows, where 'm' and 'b' stand in, respectively, for 'Max' and 'Boydy', 'B' for 'is big', and 'I' for 'is identical to'.

$$Bm, Imb \therefore Bb$$

But this form, like the simpler (though more abstract) A-B-C version above, is invalid according to all of our canvassed theories. The reason, once again, is that it is devoid of any *logically significant expressions* in terms of which the form would be counted as valid. To make the point plain: notice that, in the classical theory, we have counterexamples to the argument form. In particular, consider a case c where (to keep things simple) the domain is $\{2, 3\}$, and B is true only of object 2, and I (a binary predicate) is true only of the pair $\langle 2, 3 \rangle$, and m and b denote

2 and 3, respectively.[2] Given the truth-in-a-case conditions for atomics (see Chapter 7), we have it that $c \models_1 Imb$ and $c \models_1 Bm$ but $c \not\models_1 Bb$. Hence, we have a counterexample to the given argument form, and hence it's invalid according to the classical theory. (Since, at least for the current theories, a classical counterexample is also a counterexample in our non-classical theories, the current counterexample shows the given argument form to be invalid according to all of the theories canvassed so far.)

What you're thinking (correctly) is that there's something inappropriate about the above counterexample. In particular, the given case (the given counterexample) fails to respect *identity*: it not only errs in treating I as something that holds among non-identical objects (viz., 2 and 3); it even fails to contain all—indeed, any—*identity pairs* $\langle 1, 1 \rangle$ and $\langle 2, 2 \rangle$. What you're thinking (correctly) is that the validity of

1. Max is big.

2. Max is identical to Boydy.

3. Therefore, Boydy is big.

turns on treating 'is identical to' as *identity*. What we need, then, is an identity predicate that gets treated the right way in all cases—namely, as *identity*. And this calls for expanding our stock of logical expressions (in the syntax) and modifying our account of cases (in the semantics).

8.3 Identity: informal sketch

Following standard practice we shall recognize an *identity predicate* among our logical expressions. Our stock of logical expressions, then, shall contain logical connectives and a logical predicate.

Consider the (binary) predicate 'is identical to' in English. This predicate is generally thought to be true of all 'identity pairs', that is, true of *you and yourself, me and myself, Agnes and herself*, and so on—namely, true of all and only pairs $\langle o, o \rangle$

---

[2]In slightly more formal terms (from the formal picture of Chapter 7): $D = \{2, 3\}$, $I^+ = \{\langle 2, 3 \rangle\}$ and $B^+ = \{2\}$, and $\delta(m) = 2$ and $\delta(b) = 3$. See Chapter 7 for details of our formal cases.

for all objects *o* whatsoever. This is the main feature of identity
that we shall assume throughout.

Notice that out of the (binary) identity predicate arises a host
of unary self-identity predicates (as we might call them):[3] for each
name α, we can form 'is identical to α'. So, for example, we have
'is identical to Max', 'is identical to Boydy', and so on. The way
that identity works is that each such self-identity predicate is true
of exactly one thing: 'is identical to Max' is true of and only of
Max, and 'is identical to Boydy' is true of and only of Boydy, and
so on. Hence, 'is identical to Boydy' is true of Max if and only
if Max is, well, Boydy—that is, if and only if Max is identical
to Boydy. You can have more than one name, but you can't be
identical to more than one thing. That's just the way identity
works, at least for our purposes.

Despite treating it as a logical expression, we are not treating
identity claims as molecular: they do not contain (sentential) connectives. Still, treating identity as a logical expression, as we are
doing, requires giving it its own truth conditions—in short, specifying how identity claims are to be treated in our cases (models).
In particular, we need to put constraints on how these particular
atomic sentences (viz., our identity sentences) get to be true-in-
cases and false-in-cases.

8.4   Truth conditions: informal sketch

Our *truth-in-a-case* conditions are pretty much what you'd expect. Our cases, as in Chapter 7, come equipped with a domain
D of all objects (viz., all objects recognized by the given case), and
also are equipped with a denotation function δ, which provides
denotations for all names, and extensions and antiextensions to
all predicates.

Our concern, for now, is with atomic statements. Atomic sentences, *in general*, have the following truth conditions, where Π
is any predicate, each α_i a name, and *c* any case.

---

[3]Strictly speaking, such 'derivative predicates' will not be explicitly acknowledged in the formal picture (syntax), but we will have so-called 'open
sentences' (in Chapter 9) that play the same role. (This will become clearer
when, in Chapter 9, we add so-called object variables.)

- $\Pi\alpha_1, \ldots, \alpha_n$ is true-in-c iff in c, $\langle\delta(\alpha_1), \ldots, \delta(\alpha_n)\rangle$ is in Π's extension.
- $\Pi\alpha_1, \ldots, \alpha_n$ is false-in-c iff in c, $\langle\delta(\alpha_1), \ldots, \delta(\alpha_n)\rangle$ is in Π's antiextension.

What we want to do is simply treat identity sentences as a special case of the general clauses above: all cases give a specific (and, I hope, predictable) extension to our identity predicate. Specifically, letting '=' be our identity predicate,[4] the natural constraint on identity is a constraint on its *extension*.

- For any case c, the extension of '=' is the set of all (and only) 'identity pairs' $\langle\delta(\alpha), \delta(\alpha)\rangle$ for each object $\delta(\alpha)$ in c's domain.

In other words, the idea is just as you'd expect: that an identity claim like $m = b$ is true-in-a-case c iff whatever, according to c, is the denotation of 'm' is also what, according to c, is the denotation of 'b'. In yet other words: an identity claim is true-in-a-case just if, according to the given case, the names flanking the identity predicate denote the same object. (Hence, e.g., claims like $m = m$ are true-in-*all cases*. Why?)

But what about *falsity* conditions? What falsity clauses do we give for identity claims? There are numerous options, but we shall go with a broad, simple approach. In short, we shall leave the falsity clause for atomics alone: we'll leave it exactly as per the general clause above.

- For any case c, the antiextension of '=' is any set of pairs $\langle\delta(\alpha_i), \delta(\alpha_j)\rangle$ for any objects $\delta(\alpha_i)$ and $\delta(\alpha_j)$ in c's domain.

In other words, the identity predicate is false of a pair of objects just if that pair is in the antiextension of the predicate. That's it. Of course, if one wishes (perhaps for logical-theoretical reasons), one can mimic what we did for the extension: one can simply declare that the antiextension of identity contain *only such and so pairs*, or *never these pairs*, or—perhaps what might prima facie be very natural—comprise *all* pairs $\langle o, o'\rangle$ such that o is not identical to o' (all 'non-identity pairs', we might say). These options raise

---

[4]For familiarity's sake, we use so-called infix notation and write '$\alpha_i = \alpha_j$' instead of what we have been using (so-called prefix notation) '$= \alpha_i\alpha_j$' (e.g., as in 'Imb' above, versus 'mIb').

intriguing logical ideas, but they are left for the reader to explore. We shall assume the simple approach to identity's antiextension above.

8.5 Formal picture

There's not much more to the formal picture than what we've discussed above. The only significant change is our additional (logical) predicate, added to the syntax, and the corresponding additional semantic clauses—the truth conditions for the new predicate. Our cases remain as before, except that δ (the denotation function) now has the additional work on the identity predicate—and must treat the predicate as, well, *identity*.

Even though there is only a little bit being added to the formal picture, it will be useful to simply lay out the full picture here, and so repeat clauses from Chapter 7.

8.5.1 *Syntax*

This is just as in Chapter 7 but we now add a special (logical) predicate: a binary identity predicate '$=$'.

- A set of (non-logical) predicates:[5] $F, G, H, \ldots, S, T$ with or without numerical subscripts.
- A set of names: a, b, c, d with or without numerical subscripts.
- A *logical* (binary) predicate: $=$.

These sets, as before, expand our 'vocabulary' or 'building blocks'. We must now expand our definition of *sentences*.

1. Atomics: if Π is an n-ary predicate (logical or non-logical), and $\alpha_1, \ldots, \alpha_n$ are n many names, then $\Pi\alpha_1, \ldots, \alpha_n$ is an atomic.[6]
2. All atomics are sentences.
3. If A and B are sentences, so too are $\neg A$, $(A \wedge B)$, and $(A \vee B)$.
4. Nothing else is a sentence unless it counts as one via (1)–(3).[7]

We now move to semantics.

---

[5] Calling them *non-logical* just means that there's no special semantics for them except for what is involved in treating them as predicates of the language.

[6] We shall continue to write identity sentences in infix notation: $\alpha_i = \alpha_j$ is an atomic.

[7] We leave $\rightarrow$ and $\leftrightarrow$ as defined. See previous chapters.

8.5.2 *Semantics*

In what follows, we modify the picture from Chapter 7 only with constraints for identity (notably, specifying a constraint on the extension of identity). As in previous chapters, these clauses serve not only as truth-/falsity-in-a-case conditions; they also serve to constrain the target class of cases.

- Atomics
    * General
        $$c \models_1 \Pi\alpha_1,\ldots,\alpha_n \text{ iff } \langle\delta(\alpha_1),\ldots,\delta(\alpha_n)\rangle \in \mathcal{E}_\Pi^+.$$
        $$c \models_0 \Pi\alpha_1,\ldots,\alpha_n \text{ iff } \langle\delta(\alpha_1),\ldots,\delta(\alpha_n)\rangle \in \mathcal{E}_\Pi^-.$$
    * Logical (viz., identity)
        $$\mathcal{E}_=^+ = \{\langle\delta(\alpha),\delta(\alpha)\rangle : \delta(\alpha) \in D\}.$$
        $$\mathcal{E}_=^- \subseteq D \times D.$$

- Negations

    $c \models_1 \neg A$ iff $c \models_0 A$.

    $c \models_0 \neg A$ iff $c \models_1 A$.

- Conjunctions

    $c \models_1 A \wedge B$ iff $c \models_1 A$ and $c \models_1 B$.

    $c \models_0 A \wedge B$ iff $c \models_0 A$ or $c \models_0 B$.

- Disjunctions

    $c \models_1 A \vee B$ iff $c \models_1 A$ or $c \models_1 B$.

    $c \models_0 A \vee B$ iff $c \models_0 A$ and $c \models_0 B$.

With the above truth (and falsity) conditions, we now define consequence as usual, using the recipe from Chapter 1. For convenience, we invoke terminology from Chapter 7. We say that case c *satisfies* sentence A iff $c \models_1 A$. In turn, where $\mathcal{X}$ is a set of sentences, we say that c satisfies $\mathcal{X}$ iff c satisfies every sentence in $\mathcal{X}$. Given this terminology, we define—in effect, our glutty–gappy FDE (with identity) account of—consequence as follows.[8]

- $\mathcal{X} \vdash A$ iff any case that satisfies $\mathcal{X}$ satisfies A.

---

[8]In all subsequent theories discussed, we'll assume that we have the identity predicate in the language. So, we will not explicitly subscript the identity sign to indicate a new consequence relation, but one could write something like '$\vdash_{bc}^=$', '$\vdash_{K3}^=$', '$\vdash_{FDE}^=$', etc. if one wishes.

Note that, given the above, the argument form

$$Bm, m = b \therefore Bb$$

is now a valid form according to the general theory above. After all, a counterexample to the given form would have to be a case in which all premises are true but the conclusion Bb is untrue. But— given our semantics (in particular, constraints on identity)—any case c such that $c \models m = b$ is one in which the names b and m denote the same thing, and so the predicate B is true of the denotation of b iff true of the denotation of m. (More formally: given that $c \models_1 m = b$, we have it that $\delta(b) \in B^+$ iff $\delta(m) \in B^+$.) So, there can't be a countermodel to the given argument form.

8.6   Summary and looking ahead

Summary. We have expanded our stock of *logical expressions*. In addition to the basic connectives, we now have a logical *predicate*, namely, identity. Unlike the other (non-logical) predicates, whose extensions are unconstrained from case to case, identity's extension is governed by the same constraint across all cases: the extension comprises all and only the 'identity pairs' formed from the given domain. On the other hand, we've let the antiextension of identity be as per the general case: it's simply any set of pairs built from the domain. (One can, as the Exercises indicate, get a non-gappy or non-glutty theory—indeed, specifically, the classical logical theory—of identity by making adjustments on the antiextension.)

Looking Ahead. In the next chapter, we expand our set of logical expressions once again, but this time we add a few so-called quantifiers, in addition to variables (for objects in our domain).

Further Reading. Any standard textbook that covers so-called classical first-order logic (e.g., Smith 2003) will be a useful supplement to this chapter's topic(s); however, for the full non-classical account sketched here, a good source for further reading is Priest's textbook mentioned in previous chapters (under 'further reading'), namely, Priest 2008.

Exercises

1. What, in your own words, is the difference between a logical and non-logical expression? Why is the distinction important for specifying a logical theory (a theory's account of validity)?

2. Discuss the following argument: not everything is identical to itself. After all, I weighed less than 10 pounds when I was born, and I weigh much more than that today. If I were identical to myself, then I'd both weigh less than 10 pounds and more than 10 pounds, but this is impossible.

3. The following questions concern the broad logical theory as sketched in this (and the previous) chapter.

   (a) Can there be any case c in which $b = b$ is untrue (i.e., $c \not\models_1 b = b$)? If so, specify such a case.

   (b) Can there be any case c in which $b = b$ is false (i.e., $c \models_0 b = b$)? If so, specify such a case.

   (c) Can there be cases in which $b = c$ is neither true nor false?

   (d) Can there be cases in which $b = c$ is both true and false?

4. What constraints would you impose on cases (particularly, the antiextension of identity) to rule out 'gappy' identity claims (where an identity claim is gappy in a case iff neither it nor its negation is true-in-the-given-case)?

5. What constraints would you impose on cases to rule out 'glutty' identity claims (where an identity claim is glutty in a case iff both it and its negation are true-in-the-given-case)?

6. What constraints would you impose on cases to ensure that (as per classical thinking) every identity sentence is either true or false but not both (i.e., true-in-a-case or false-in-a-case, but not both)?

Sample answers

Answer 4. First, notice that some identity claims can never be gappy since they are true-in-*all cases*: namely, all of those identity claims of the form $\alpha = \alpha$. (A glance at the constraints on the extension of '=' shows that $\alpha = \alpha$ is true-in-*all of our cases*, for any name α.) On the other hand, we can get gappy identity claims that involve more than one name (e.g., $a = b$ or the like). (See your answer to Exercise 3.c above.) To remove such gaps from identity claims, we simply demand that, for every case c, the union of the extension and antiextension of identity (i.e., of '=') contains all ordered pairs from the c's domain; in other words, we impose $\mathcal{E}_=^+ \cup \mathcal{E}_=^- = D \times D$. (If you've forgotten your set-theoretic notions, you should turn back to Chapter 3 for a refresher!) With this constraint on the identity predicate, there can be no pair $\langle x, y \rangle$ of objects, with x and y from D, that's in neither the extension nor antiextension of the identity predicate. And this, given the definition of *truth in a case* and *falsity in a case*, ensures that identity claims cannot be gappy.

9

Everything and Something

Try to learn something about everything
and everything about something.
– Thomas H. Huxley

The previous chapter introduced a slightly richer language by giving some structure to our atomics. In this chapter, we enrich the language some more, this time by adding a few more logical devices—in particular, the existential and universal quantifiers. The addition of quantifiers, in turn, requires the addition of so-called individual variables (variables ranging over objects). Despite such additional items, we needn't alter our basic, expanded idea of 'cases' from Chapter 7.[1] We will begin with a few informal remarks to motivate the quantifiers, and then rely on Chapter 7 to briefly sketch the formal picture.

9.1   Validity involving quantifiers

The chief aim of logic, as you know, is consequence. The aim is to give an account (a logical theory) of what follows from what in our language (or some fragment thereof). All of our basic logical theories, so far, agree on the validity of numerous argument forms.[2] For example, all of the given theories would classify the following argument as valid.

1. Max is happy and Agnes is sleeping.
2. Therefore, Agnes is sleeping.

Given our enriched account of atomics from Chapter 7, we can think of this argument as having the form: $Hm \land Sa \therefore Sa$. It

---

[1] This is partly because we will make a simplifying assumption concerning available names. (We will skip a detour through so-called satisfaction, which is due to Tarski.)

[2] Of course, they disagree on various forms too, which is why they're different theories.

is clear, from Chapter 7, that such an argument form is valid in FDE (our general paraconsistent theory), and hence in both K3 (our gappy-but-non-glutty theory) and the classical theory.[3] If $c \models_1 Hm \land Sa$ then $c \models_1 Hm$ and $c \models_1 Sa$ by the conjunction truth conditions.

There are (many) other argument forms that all three logical theories take to be valid. On the other hand, what about the following argument?

3. Every cat is smart.

4. Agnes is a cat.

5. Therefore, Agnes is smart.

On the surface, one would think that this argument is valid. After all, how could (3) and (4) be true without (5) being true? It's hard to imagine how that could be so. As such, one would think that, whatever our 'cases' might be like, an accurate logical theory of our language should count the given argument as valid.

As it turns out, our basic logical theories, given their minimal set of logical connectives, cannot count the given argument, from (3) and (4) to (5), as valid. To see this, recall that our basic theories recognize only conjunction, disjunction, and negation—along with the derived conditional and biconditional—among its connectives. Do any of these connectives appear in the above argument? No. As such, the given argument contains only *atomic* sentences, at least if our connectives are only the given basic ones. In effect, it has the form $p, q \therefore r$, which, as you can establish, is invalid on all of our basic theories.

You might think that the form $p, q \therefore r$ is not digging deeply enough. After all, we now have predicates and names. As such, (4) and (5) can be more accurately represented by (say) Ca and Sa, respectively. The question, however, concerns (3). What is *its* form? While 'is smart' is certainly a predicate in English, there's no obvious candidate for a *name* in (3). Whatever else it might be, 'Every cat' is not a name!

---

[3] Since FDE contains all of the K3 and classical cases, if there's no FDE case in which the premise is true and conclusion not true, then there's no such K3 or classical case either.

9.2   Quantifiers: an informal sketch

It is at this stage that a recognition of *quantifiers* emerges. In English, 'every' and 'some' serve as quantifiers—at least in the contexts of present interest, including the argument above. How are these to be understood?

There are many sorts of quantifiers in English. We will look at two of the simplest—but logically very important—quantifiers, namely, the so-called *universal* and *existential* quantifiers.

In effect, quantifiers specify a *quantity* of objects. The universal quantifier is so-called because it specifies *all* or *every* object. The existential (or, traditionally, particular) quantifier is so-called because it specifies *some* object (or other)—at least one object.

It is standard to let $\forall$ and $\exists$ represent our universal and existential quantifiers, respectively. Such quantifiers are said to *range* over a given domain (in effect, the domain of all objects). To make things easier, we introduce individual variables to play the role that the term 'object' plays in 'Every object is physical' or 'Some object is non-physical' or the like. As such, we never write '$\forall$' or '$\exists$' without some individual (or object) variable. Instead, we write, for example, '$\forall x$', or '$\forall y$', or '$\exists z$', or '$\exists x$', or etc., where 'x', 'y', and 'z' serve as our object variables. Given a variable (say, 'x'), '$\forall x$' may be read *every object x is such that* ..., while '$\exists x$' is read *there is at least one object x such that*...

Consider two (so-called unrestricted) examples, say,

6. Everything is happy.
7. Something is a cat.

On standard readings, logicians read (6) and (7) as follows.[4]

6'. Every object x is such that x is happy.
7'. Some object x (or other) is such that x is a cat.

In fact, the word 'object' can be dropped, since it is understood that 'x' is ranging over objects. So, one could equally write

6''. Every x is such that x is happy.
7''. Some x (or other) is such that x is a cat.

---

[4] Note that it doesn't matter *which* (object) variable you use here; it's just important to use some such variable or other.

Let H serve for our (unary) predicate 'is happy', and C for 'is a cat'. Given as much, (6) and (7) would generally be formalized as follows.

F6. $\forall x H x$

F7. $\exists x C x$

9.3 Truth and falsity conditions

Our 'cases' are as in Chapter 7. Recall that cases now come equipped with a domain D of objects (viz., all objects that exist, according to the given case). Cases also provide denotations for all names, and extensions and antiextensions to all predicates.

The natural truth and falsity conditions are what you'd expect on brief reflection, but they're slightly easier to give once we get clearer on the official syntax. (See next section.) For now, we'll simply wave at the basic idea, leaving some of the essential terminology undefined.

Quantifiers are tied to variables. So, in general (though loosely speaking), a universally quantified sentence may be thought of as having something of the structure '$\forall v(\ldots v \ldots)$', where v is some (object) variable. Similarly, an existentially quantified sentence may be thought of as having something of the form '$\exists v(\ldots v \ldots)$'. Now, the '$\ldots v \ldots$' can be thought of as a condition of sorts. As such, '$\forall v(\ldots v \ldots)$' says, in effect, that every object satisfies the condition '$\ldots v \ldots$', while '$\exists v(\ldots v \ldots)$' says that some object (or other) satisfies the given condition.

So, in effect, the basic idea is that $c \models_1 \forall v(\ldots v \ldots)$ iff every object in c's domain D satisfies the condition $\ldots v \ldots$ In turn, $c \models_0 \forall v(\ldots v \ldots)$ iff some object in c's domain D fails to satisfy the condition $\ldots v \ldots$.

Similarly, $c \models_1 \exists v(\ldots v \ldots)$ iff some object in c's domain D satisfies the condition $\ldots v \ldots$. In turn, $c \models_0 \exists v(\ldots v \ldots)$ iff no object in c's domain D satisfies the condition $\ldots v \ldots$ (i.e., every object in the domain fails to satisfy the given condition).

This is all fairly intuitive, but it requires a clear account of what 'satisfaction' means. We will officially skip this, and take a slightly different approach. In particular, we will assume that every object in the domain (of any case) has a name in our language. This allows us to give natural truth and falsity conditions for the quantifiers without a detour through the somewhat involved notion of 'satisfaction'. In effect, we simply define the idea of an *instance* of some 'condition'. In particular, where . . . v . . . is some 'condition',[5] an *instance* of . . . v . . . is the result of replacing all occurrences of v with some name (using the same name for every occurrence of the same variable).[6] With this in mind, we can just say

- Existential sentences

  ∃v(. . . v . . .) is true-in-*c* iff . . . v . . . is true of some object in *D*.

  ∃v(. . . v . . .) is false-in-*c* iff . . . v . . . is false of every object in *D*.

- Universal sentences

  ∀v(. . . v . . .) is true-in-*c* iff . . . v . . . is true of every object in *D*.

  ∀v(. . . v . . .) is false-in-*c* iff . . . v . . . is false of some object in *D*.

We turn to the formal picture, where this becomes clearer.

9.4   A formal picture

As above, our cases are as in Chapter 7, except that now we stipulate that all objects in the domain (of any case) have a name in the language. We will present the broad, paraconsistent (and paracomplete) theory. As in Chapter 7, one gets the classical or (non-paraconsistent) paracomplete theory by putting restrictions on the extensions and antiextensions of predicates.

9.4.1   *Syntax*

The syntax is now slightly more involved. We add individual or object variables, and we add the two new quantifiers. In addition, for convenience, we have to introduce a few new syntactic categories (e.g., 'term', 'open sentence', etc.).

In addition to the older ingredients, we add (with some repetition from Chapter 7) the following.

- A set of object variables: x, y, z with or without numerical subscripts.

- A set of (non-logical) predicates: $F, G, H, \ldots, S, T$ with or without numerical subscripts.

---

[5]Such 'conditions' will be called *open sentences* in the formal picture.

[6]Strictly speaking, one needs to replace all so-called *free* variables in the condition. This is easier to state in the formal setting, so we'll skip that here.

- A set of names: a, b, c, d with or without numerical subscripts.
- A *logical* (binary) predicate: =.
- Two quantifiers: $\forall$ and $\exists$.

For convenience, we define a *term* to be either a variable or a name.

Before we define our *sentences*, it is useful to detour through a definition of *formulas* (expressions of the language that count as 'well-formed' but need not be full sentences).

- Atomic Formulas: if Π is an n-ary predicate, and $\tau_1, \ldots, \tau_n$ are *terms* (names or variables), then $\Pi\tau_1, \ldots, \tau_n$ is an atomic formula.[7]
- All atomic formulas are formulas.
- If A and B are formulas, then $\neg A$, $(A \wedge B)$, and $(A \vee B)$ are formulas.[8]
- If A is any formula and v any variable, then $\forall\mathsf{v}A$ and $\exists\mathsf{v}A$ are formulas.
- Nothing else (except the above defined) is a formula.

With formulas so defined, we can now define the notion of an *open formula* (or 'open sentence'). First, we say that an occurrence of a variable v is *bound* iff it occurs in a context $\forall\mathsf{v}\ldots\mathsf{v}\ldots$ or $\exists\mathsf{v}\ldots\mathsf{v}\ldots$.[9] In effect, bound variables are always 'tied' to a quantifier. We say that v is *free* in a formula iff it is not bound. With this in mind, we can concisely specify our set of sentences:

- A is a *sentence* of our new language iff it is a formula with no free variables.

Let us turn to the semantics.

9.4.2 *Semantics*

Our cases, as above, are as in Chapter 7. In particular, a case is a structure $\langle D, \delta \rangle$ where D is the domain and δ provides denota-

---

[7]We continue to use infix notation for identity formulas, writing '$\alpha_i = \alpha_j$' (instead of the prefix notation '$= \alpha_i\alpha_j$').

[8]We also have both $(A \rightarrow B)$ and $(A \leftrightarrow B)$ as defined formulas (see previous chapters on how we define these).

[9]There is a precise way of defining *bound variable*, but it is tedious, and herein skipped.

tions of all names, and provides extensions and antiextensions to all predicates. The new stipulation, as above, is that all objects of the domain (of any case) have a name in our language.

The stipulation about names allows us to introduce the following notation, which will be used in giving the truth (and falsity) conditions for quantified sentences. In particular, where $A(\mathsf{v})$ is any open formula (see above), we let $A(\alpha/\mathsf{v})$ be the result of replacing all occurrences of v in $A(\mathsf{v})$ with the name α. For example, let $A(x)$ be the open formula $Fx \lor \exists y Gy$. (Notice that 'y' is bound in the formula, and that only 'x' is free.) In this context, $A(b/x)$ is the sentence (closed formula) $Fb \lor \exists y Gy$. You can think of other examples. Notice that $A(\alpha/\mathsf{v})$ is (in effect) an *instance* of $A(\mathsf{v})$, as we used the term above.

Retaining the notation from Chapter 7, we can now give the truth and falsity conditions for all of our sentences. For convenience, the conditions for atomics and non-quantified sentences (from Chapter 8) are repeated here.[10]

- Atomics
  * General
    $$c \models_1 \Pi\alpha_1, \ldots, \alpha_n \text{ iff } \langle \delta(\alpha_1), \ldots, \delta(\alpha_n) \rangle \in \mathcal{E}_\Pi^+.$$
    $$c \models_0 \Pi\alpha_1, \ldots, \alpha_n \text{ iff } \langle \delta(\alpha_1), \ldots, \delta(\alpha_n) \rangle \in \mathcal{E}_\Pi^-.$$
  * Logical (viz., Identity)
    $$\mathcal{E}_=^+ = \{ \langle \delta(\alpha), \delta(\alpha) \rangle : \delta(\alpha) \in D \}.$$
    $$\mathcal{E}_=^- \subseteq D \times D.$$
- Negations
  $c \models_1 \neg A$ iff $c \models_0 A$
  $c \models_0 \neg A$ iff $c \models_1 A$
- Conjunctions
  $c \models_1 A \land B$ iff $c \models_1 A$ and $c \models_1 B$
  $c \models_0 A \land B$ iff $c \models_0 A$ or $c \models_0 B$
- Disjunctions
  $c \models_1 A \lor B$ iff $c \models_1 A$ or $c \models_1 B$
  $c \models_0 A \lor B$ iff $c \models_0 A$ and $c \models_0 B$

---

[10]We give truth and falsity conditions only for *sentences*, not open formulas. (There are standard ways of giving 'truth conditions' for open formulas that, in effect, treat the free variables as names. We ignore this for simplicity.)

- Universal sentences

  $c \models_1 \forall \mathsf{v} A$ iff $c \models_1 A(\alpha/\mathsf{v})$ for all α such that $\delta(\alpha) \in D$.[11]

  $c \models_0 \forall \mathsf{v} A$ iff $c \models_0 A(\alpha/\mathsf{v})$ for some α such that $\delta(\alpha) \in D$.

- Existential sentences

  $c \models_1 \exists \mathsf{v} A$ iff $c \models_1 A(\alpha/\mathsf{v})$ for some α such that $\delta(\alpha) \in D$.

  $c \models_0 \exists \mathsf{v} A$ iff $c \models_0 A(\alpha/\mathsf{v})$ for all α such that $\delta(\alpha) \in D$.

With the above truth and falsity conditions, we can now define consequence as usual. To make things general, we say that case c *satisfies* sentence A iff $c \models_1 A$. In turn, where $\mathcal{X}$ is a set of sentences, we say that c satisfies $\mathcal{X}$ iff c satisfies every sentence in $\mathcal{X}$. Given this terminology, we define—in effect, our glutty–gappy FDE (with quantifiers) account of—consequence as follows.

- $\mathcal{X} \vdash A$ iff any case that satisfies $\mathcal{X}$ satisfies A.

« *Parenthetical remark.* Note that our existential quantifier, combined with identity, may be used to express existence claims. In particular, we can take claims like '*b* exists' to have the logical form $\exists x(x = b)$, which is true (in a case) just if (the object named) *b* exists (in the case)—just if, that is, $\delta(b) \in D$. (Recall that the domain D, in a case, comprises everything that exists according to the given case.) This topic is discussed further in the next chapter. *End remark.* »

9.5   Paraconsistent, paracomplete, classical

By now, you should recognize that the foregoing account, without further constraint, is our broad, paraconsistent (and paracomplete) account. To get our non-paraconsistent, paracomplete account, one adds only the Exclusion constraint on extensions and antiextensions (see Chapter 7). To get the classical account, one adds, in addition to Exclusion, the Exhaustion constraint.

---

[11]Here, as in the case for existentials (below), α is a name in our language (and we've stipulated that everything in the domain of c has a name α_i in our language, for any case c (and that, in turn, δ assigns a name $\delta(\alpha_i)$ to each name in the language). NB: the clause 'such that $\delta(\alpha) \in D$' is not necessary, but it is useful for later discussion (see Chapter 10).

9.6 Summary and looking ahead

Summary. We have introduced the universal and existential quantifiers, and now have a much richer language. In addition to affording 'general talk' about something (or other) and everything (or nothing), our quantifiers also give some sense to outright existence claims: saying that *Max exists* may be formalized as $\exists x(x = \text{Max})$.

Looking Ahead. But what about 'objects' that *don't* exist—but about which we can still truly or falsely speak? This topic is briefly addressed in the next chapter, wherein we 'free up' our names.

Further Reading. As with the last few chapters, any standard textbook that covers so-called classical first-order logic will be a useful supplement to this chapter's topic(s); however, for the full non-classical account sketched here, a good source for further reading is Priest's textbook mentioned in previous chapters (under 'further reading').

Exercises

1. Consider a case $c = \langle D, \delta \rangle$ where $D = \{1, 2, 3\}$ and $\delta(a) = 1$, $\delta(b) = 2$, and $\delta(d) = 3$, and $F^+ = \{2, 3\}$ and $F^- = \{1\}$. Additionally, where R is a binary predicate, let $R^+ = \{\langle 1, 2 \rangle, \langle 1, 1 \rangle\}$ and $R^- = \{\langle 1, 1 \rangle, \langle 1, 2 \rangle, \langle 1, 3 \rangle\}$. For each of the following, say whether it is true or false. If true, say why. If false, say why.

   (a) $c \models_1 \forall x F x$
   (b) $c \models_0 \forall x F x$
   (c) $c \models_1 \exists x F x$
   (d) $c \models_0 \exists x F x$
   (e) $c \models_1 \forall x R x b$
   (f) $c \models_0 \forall x R x b$
   (g) $c \models_1 \exists x R a x$
   (h) $c \models_0 \exists x R a x$
   (i) $c \models_1 \forall x (R a b \rightarrow F x)$
   (j) $c \models_1 \exists x \forall y R x y$
   (k) $c \models_1 \neg \exists x \forall y R x y$
   (l) $c \models_0 \forall x \exists y R x y$

2. Construct a case in which $\forall x Gx \lor \forall x \neg Gx$ is not true.[12]

3. Give a case in which $\forall x(Gx \to Hx)$ is true but $\forall x(Gx \land Hx)$ is not true.

4. The argument from §9.1 about Agnes and cats, from (3) and (4) to (5), has the form $\forall x(Cx \to Sx), Ca \therefore Sa$. In which of our three logical theories is this argument valid? (Give a counterexample for any theory in which the argument is invalid.)

5. Which of the following best expresses that *nothing is horrible*? Justify your answer by appealing to the truth and falsity conditions of the quantifiers.

    (a) $\neg \forall x Hx$
    (b) $\neg \exists x Hx$

6. Do the two-way-validity claims hold in our current paraconsistent (and paracomplete) theory with quantifiers—a theory we'll call 'FDE' (even though we now have quantifiers)? Justify your answer.

    (a) $\forall x Fx \dashv\vdash \neg \exists x \neg Fx$
    (b) $\exists x Fx \dashv\vdash \neg \forall x \neg Fx$

Sample answers

Answer 1a. Claim (1a) is false: $\forall x Fx$ is not true-in-our given case. To show as much, we invoke the truth conditions for the universal quantifier, which has it that $c \models_1 \forall x Fx$ iff $c \models_1 F\alpha$ for all names α such that $\delta(\alpha) \in D$. Hence, if each of Fa, Fb, and Fd are true-in-our given c, then so too is $\forall x Fx$. To figure out whether these (atomic) sentences are true, we need to consult the truth conditions for atomics. Quick consultation reveals that Fa is true in c iff $\delta(a)$ is in F^+. But $\delta(a) = 1$, and $1 \notin F^+$. Hence, $c \not\models_1 Fa$, and so, as above, $c \not\models_1 \forall x Fx$.

Answer 1b. Claim (1b) is true: $\forall x Fx$ is false-in-our-given-c. The falsity conditions (i.e., conditions for $\models_0$) for the universal quantifier tell us that $c \models_0 \forall x Fx$ if any of Fa, Fb, or Fd are false-in-c.

---

[12] As in Chapter 7, to construct a case, you have to specify the domain, the denotations of the various names, and the extension and antiextensions of given predicates.

Figuring out whether any of these (atomic) sentences is false-in-c involves consulting the falsity conditions for atomics. Quick consultation reveals that Fa is false-in-c iff $\delta(a)$ is in F^-. But $\delta(a) = 1$, and $1 \in F^-$. Hence, $c \models_0 Fa$, and so, as above, $c \models_0 \forall x Fx$.

Answer 1c. The truth conditions for the existential quantifier tell us that $c \models_1 \exists x Fx$ iff either Fa, Fb or Fd is true-in-c. Truth conditions for these atomics reveals that $c \models_1 Fb$ (similarly for Fd) since $\delta(b) = 2$ and $2 \in F^+$ (similarly, $\delta(d) = 3$ and $3 \in F^+$). So, claim (1c) is true: $c \models_1 \exists x Fx$.

Answer 1d. The falsity conditions for the existential quantifier tell us that $c \models_0 \exists x Fx$ iff each of Fa, Fb, and Fd is false-in-c. Falsity conditions for these atomics reveals that $c \not\models_0 Fb$ (similarly for Fd) since $\delta(b) = 2$ but $2 \notin F^-$ (similarly for d with $3 \notin F^-$). So, claim (1d) is false: $c \not\models_0 \exists x Fx$.

Answer 1l. Claim (1l) is true: $\forall x \exists y Rxy$ is false-in-our-given-case. By the falsity conditions for the universal quantifier, we have that $c \models_0 \forall x \exists y Rxy$ if and only if $c \models_0 \exists y R\alpha y$ for some name α such that $\delta(\alpha) \in D$. Is there such a name α such that $c \models_0 \exists y R\alpha y$? Yes: the name a fits the bill: $c \models_0 \exists y Ray$. After all, by the falsity conditions for the existential quantifier, $c \models_0 \exists y Ray$ iff $c \models_0 Ra\alpha$ for all names α (such that $\delta(\alpha) \in D$). So, $c \models_0 \exists y Ray$ iff $c \models_0 Raa$ and $c \models_0 Rab$ and $c \models_0 Rad$. But that's exactly what we have in our given case: each of Raa, Rab and Rad is indeed false-in-c, since $\delta(a) = 1$, $\delta(b) = 2$, $\delta(d) = 3$, and the antiextension of R contains each of the pairs $\langle 1, 1 \rangle$, $\langle 1, 2 \rangle$, and $\langle 1, 3 \rangle$.

PART IV

FREEDOM, NECESSITY, AND BEYOND

10

Speaking Freely

Imaginary characters don't exist.
— Guy Stewart

In this chapter we 'free up' our names by unloading their so-called existential import (a term explained below). We do this by slightly expanding our account of cases (or models)—in particular, adding a special subset of our domains—and, in turn, restricting our quantifiers to the new special subset. Such adjustments are required to accommodate a sort of 'freedom of speech' (though not in any legal sense of the term).[1]

10.1 Speaking of non-existent 'things'

We can and often do talk about all manner of things, even those things that are merely imaginary—various things that don't in fact exist. Consider my imaginary friend Guy Stewart (or Guy, as some call him). You never have and never will see Guy, since Guy is invisible to the human eye. But Guy knows what you look like, and in fact knows all about you—and, indeed, knows all about everything; Guy is omniscient.

I could go on and on about Guy, about how fun and interesting he is, and so on. I'm sure that you'd like him, and like learning more and more about him. But time and page space is limited.

For present purposes, what is important is not so much what you know or believe about Guy; what's important is that you've at least thought about Guy. Indeed, you're probably still thinking about Guy. But now note: in thinking about Guy you're thinking about something (viz., Guy), but the something about which you're thinking does not exist. Guy, after all, is imaginary.

---

[1]Let me emphasize that this chapter presents only one sort of motivation for (some versions of) so-called free logic. Readers, as for all chapters, are encouraged to pursue further reading.

10.2   Existential import

A name α carries *existential import*—or is *existentially loaded*—
just if there is something named α that exists (just if, in other
words, the name denotes some existing object).[2] What Guy Stewart teaches us is that, apparently, some names are not existentially loaded; some predicates (e.g., 'Agnes is thinking about x',
'x is imaginary') can be true of some 'things' that don't exist
(e.g., Guy). As above, the sentence

1. Guy Stewart is imaginary.

is true even though 'Guy Stewart' fails to denote any existing
object. Accordingly, sentence (1) does not imply

2. There is some existent object x such that x is Guy Stewart.

But, now, we see the need to expand our Chapter 8 account of
names and quantifiers—and free up our names.

As noted (in passing) in Chapter 9, we take existence claims

$$\alpha \text{ exists}$$

to have the form

$$\exists x(x = \alpha)$$

The logical theories in Chapter 8, then, involve an existentially
loaded account of names: such theories, one and all, treat the
argument form from $\Pi\alpha$ to $\exists v(v = \alpha)$ as valid, for any name
α, variable v, and predicate Π. But, as above, a natural lesson
to draw from Guy Stewart is that this argument form is not
ultimately valid.

« *Parenthetical remark.* You might be wondering why we don't
treat 'exists' as a regular, quantifier-free predicate in some fashion. This issue, partly for space reasons, is left open, but is well
worth your reflection. (See the exercises, where you're explicitly
asked to explore the topic and come up with your own account.)
End parenthetical. »

---

[2]Relativized to *cases*, we can say that a name α is existentially loaded *in
case c* if and only if $c \models_1 \exists x(x = \alpha)$.

10.3 Freeing our terms, expanding our domains

What we want to do is free up our terms. What we want to acknowledge are cases in which some names (e.g., 'Guy Stewart') are 'free', cases in which such names fail to denote an existing object. One way of thinking about this is as follows.

Recall from Chapter 8 that our cases are (or are modeled by) structures $\langle D, \delta \rangle$. In such cases, the domain D is thought of as comprising all that exists: to exist in such cases is just to be in D. The quantifiers $\exists$ and $\forall$ are interpreted in terms of D. In particular, for any such case c, we have that $\exists vA$ is true-in-case-c just if $A(\alpha/v)$ is true-in-c for some name α such that $\delta(\alpha)$ exists according to c (i.e., such that $\delta(\alpha)$ is in domain D).[3]

Now, perhaps the easiest way to free up our terms is to restrict our quantifiers to 'only the existent objects' in the domain. In particular, to each case we add a special—possibly empty though not necessarily proper—subset E of D, giving us slightly modified structures $\langle D, E, \delta \rangle$ that, as it were, wear their 'existential features' on their sleeves. Here, D continues to be non-empty and comprises *all objects* (of any manner) in the given case; but E comprises only the *objects that exist* in the given case. (Intuitively, Guy Stewart would go in D—and, hence, is available to think about and so on—but not in E.) In turn, the quantifiers are interpreted *not* via D, but rather only via E. In effect: all stays as before except that the truth conditions for quantifiers invoke E instead of D.

10.4 Truth conditions: an informal sketch

As above, we leave all truth (falsity) conditions the same *except* for the quantifiers. In particular, atomics and basic compounds— that is, atomic and molecular sentences involving only the basic connectives—have exactly the truth conditions from before (see Chapter 7).[4] The difference—the *freedom*—shows up in the truth

---

[3] As in Chapter 8, $A(\alpha/v)$ is the result of replacing all (free) occurrences of variable v in formula A by name α. Recall, too, that we assume—and (for simplicity) shall assume throughout—that all objects in D have names α in our given language.

[4] This sort of (so-called positive) approach to free logic is not the only approach. On other approaches (some of which are hinted at in exercises),

conditions for quantifiers, which, informally put, run roughly as follows.[5]

- Existential sentences

  $\exists v(\ldots v \ldots)$ is true-in-c iff $\ldots v \ldots$ is true of some object in E.

  $\exists v(\ldots v \ldots)$ is false-in-c iff $\ldots v \ldots$ is false of every object in E.

- Universal sentences

  $\forall v(\ldots v \ldots)$ is true-in-c iff $\ldots v \ldots$ is true of every object in E.

  $\forall v(\ldots v \ldots)$ is false-in-c iff $\ldots v \ldots$ is false of some object in E.

The idea, as above, is that our quantifiers range only over what exists. In any given case, E comprises the objects that, according to the given case, exist. Of course, in any given case, D comprises whatever objects can be talked about (or, if you like, thought about, etc.). In some cases, D contains Guy Stewart-like entities, 'objects' that we can talk (truly or falsely) about but, according to the given case, don't exist. Hence, if b is 'Guy Stewart', and I is 'imaginary', we don't want it to follow from the truth of *Guy is imaginary* that *Guy exists*; we don't want $\exists x(x = b)$ to follow from Ib.

As throughout the book, we define *consequence* as absence of counterexample, where a counterexample is a *case* in which all premises are true but the conclusion untrue. Our cases—our 'free cases', as it were—are just like the cases of Chapter 8 but now have an additional 'existence set' E in terms of which our quantifiers are interpreted. In particular, truth (and falsity) conditions for atomics like Ib and $b = b$ are just as before. So, for any 'free case' c, the sentence Ib is true in c if and only if $\delta(b)$ is in the extension of I. Moreover, identity claims are treated exactly as before, and so $b = b$ is true-in-every 'free case' c since the extension of identity claims remains as before, namely, the

---

we would need to adjust truth conditions for atomics.

[5] Here, we use a variation of notation and notions from Chapter 7. Strictly speaking, we haven't defined what it is for a 'condition' to be true of an object, and we do not use this sort of idea in the formal picture. Doing so is not overly difficult, but it complicates matters more than this 'basics' book is intended to do. We here rely on the informal idea that we've assumed (without explaining) throughout: the idea of a predicate's being true of an object. (E.g., the condition $\ldots$ *is reading* is true of you, etc.)

set of all 'identity pairs' *formed out of D*.[6] Accordingly, while the argument

$$Ib \therefore \exists x(x = b)$$

is valid in our previous existentially loaded theories (e.g., Chapter 8), our new 'free cases' give us counterexamples. A counterexample to the given argument is one in which nothing in E is in the extension of I (i.e., the predicate I isn't true of anything in E) but something—say, Guy Stewart qua denotation of b—is in the extension of I. In this case, the condition $x = b$ is true of $\delta(b)$ (i.e., the denotation of name b) but, since $\delta(b)$ is not in E, the existential claim $\exists x(x = b)$ (i.e., that b exists) is not true. But since $\delta(b)$ is in the extension of I, the sentence Ib is true-in-the-given-case. Hence, the premise is true-in-the-given-case but the conclusion untrue-in-the-case, and so we have a counterexample.

Matters are made much clearer by a formal picture of our new 'freedom', to which picture we now briefly turn.

10.5 Formal picture

The formal picture is only a slight variation on that of Chapter 9, and so we can be brief.

10.5.1 *Syntax*

The syntax is exactly that of Chapter 9 (with identity as the only logical predicate). If we wanted, we could add a distinguished (logical) existence predicate, but we need not do this. On the current approach, we can, as mentioned above, take existence claims of the forms α *exists* to be of the form $\exists x(x = \alpha)$. In general, then, we can think of the existence predicate—or, strictly, open formula—to be $\exists x(x = y)$, where y is the open variable, and so we needn't add any additional vocabulary to the syntax.

10.5.2 *Semantics*

The semantic picture, as discussed above, is basically the same as Chapter 8, except for adding a special 'existence' subset of the

---

[6]Note that we are not requiring that the extension of the identity predicate draws its pairs from E. Some free logics do this, but—to avoid further complexity—we avoid it here.

domain. Our cases are now structures $\langle D, E, \delta \rangle$, where $D \neq \emptyset$ and $E \subseteq D$. Intuitively, D comprises all objects in a particular case, while E comprises all and only the objects that, according to the given case, *exist*. (Note well: E, unlike D, may be empty.) The role of δ is exactly as in Chapters 7–8: it supplies the given case with denotations of all predicates and names. Where α is a name, $\delta(\alpha) \in D$.

While the only notable change in the formal truth (and falsity) conditions involves the quantifiers (and, in turn, involves the only additional element E in our cases), we nonetheless lay out all of the conditions here for convenience. As in Chapter 9, α is any name, and we assume that everything in the domain (of any case) has a name α_i in the language, and $A(\alpha/\mathsf{v})$ is the result of replacing all (free) occurrences of v in A with the name α.

- Atomics
  * General
    $$c \models_1 \Pi\alpha_1, \ldots, \alpha_n \text{ iff } \langle \delta(\alpha_1), \ldots, \delta(\alpha_n) \rangle \in \mathcal{E}_\Pi^+.$$
    $$c \models_0 \Pi\alpha_1, \ldots, \alpha_n \text{ iff } \langle \delta(\alpha_1), \ldots, \delta(\alpha_n) \rangle \in \mathcal{E}_\Pi^-.$$
  * Logical (viz., Identity)
    $$\mathcal{E}_=^+ = \{ \langle \delta(\alpha), \delta(\alpha) \rangle : \delta(\alpha) \in D \}.$$
    $$\mathcal{E}_=^- \subseteq D \times D.$$

- Basic connectives

  $c \models_1 \neg A$ iff $c \models_0 A$.
  $c \models_0 \neg A$ iff $c \models_1 A$.

  $c \models_1 A \vee B$ iff $c \models_1 A$ or $c \models_1 B$.
  $c \models_0 A \vee B$ iff $c \models_0 A$ and $c \models_0 B$.

  $c \models_1 A \wedge B$ iff $c \models_1 A$ and $c \models_1 B$.
  $c \models_0 A \wedge B$ iff $c \models_0 A$ or $c \models_0 B$.

- Quantifiers

  $c \models_1 \exists\mathsf{v}A$ iff $c \models_1 A(\alpha/\mathsf{v})$ for some α such that $\delta(\alpha) \in E$.
  $c \models_0 \exists\mathsf{v}A$ iff $c \models_0 A(\alpha/\mathsf{v})$ for all α such that $\delta(\alpha) \in E$.

  $c \models_1 \forall\mathsf{v}A$ iff $c \models_1 A(\alpha/\mathsf{v})$ for all α such that $\delta(\alpha) \in E$.
  $c \models_0 \forall\mathsf{v}A$ iff $c \models_0 A(\alpha/\mathsf{v})$ for some α such that $\delta(\alpha) \in E$.

We define *consequence* as we have throughout: absence of counterexample, where a counterexample is now any such 'free case' in which the premises are true and conclusion not true.

10.5.3 *A few remarks*

Notice that while every identity claim of the form

$$\alpha = \alpha$$

is logically true (i.e., true-in-*all cases*) on the current (free) theory,[7] it is no longer logically true that something *exists*, at least in the sense that sentences of the form

$$\exists x(x = \alpha)$$

are not logically true. And in this respect, at least, we have some freedom.

Moreover, as indicated above, the situation with Guy Stewart is as it should be. In particular, from *Guy is imaginary*—or from the fact that you are thinking about Guy—it does not follow that Guy exists. Our free theory (like any free theory) rejects so-called Existential Generalization, which (in effect) maintains that if something satisfies a predicate, then that thing exists. But Guy (and his ilk) seem to invalidate this. In our formal picture, a counterexample to the argument form

$$\Pi\alpha \therefore \exists\mathsf{v}(\mathsf{v} = \alpha)$$

is a case $c = \langle D, E, \delta \rangle$ such that $D = \{1\}$ and $E = \emptyset$ and $\delta(\alpha) \in \Pi^+$. Since the denotation of α is in the extension of Π, we have $c \models_1 \Pi\alpha$ but, since $\delta(\alpha)$ does not exist in c (since not in E), we have $c \not\models_1 \exists\mathsf{v}(\mathsf{v} = \alpha)$.

Summary and looking ahead

Summary. Imaginary objects like Guy Stewart don't exist, but we can also truly say as much. We can truly say as much by asserting a non-existence claim of the form $\neg\exists x(x = \text{Guy})$. And

---

[7] As noted before, alternative (e.g., so-called negative and neutral) approaches to 'freedom' do not have the logical truth of all identity claims.

we can do this by enjoying 'free names', that is, names that are not existentially loaded—they don't imply that some *existing* object bears the given name.

To accommodate all of this, we expand our cases by recognizing an *existence domain* within each case: the standard domain D comprises *all* objects recognized by the given case (including objects that, according to the given case, don't exist), and subset E of D that contains only the objects that, according to the given case, exist.

Looking Forward. In the next chapter, we expand our horizons a bit more by looking at the notions of *broad possibility* and *broad necessity*. These notions are involved in many important philosophical arguments, but also in ordinary musings (e.g., in thinking about whether Guy Stewart is *necessarily* non-existent or only *possibly* so).

Further Reading. Useful and state-of-the-art discussions of free logic are provided in essays by Ermanno Bencivenga and Scott Lehmann in Volume 5 (published in 2005) of the Gabbay & Günthner multi-volume *Handbook of Philosophical Logic* (see bibliography). An excellent collection of essays by one of the pioneers of free logic is Lambert 2003.

Exercises

1. Is the following argument valid in our 'freed up' theory? Explain your answer.[8]

$$\forall x Fx \therefore Pb \to Fb$$

   (Hint: don't forget about cases where $\delta(b) \notin E$!)

2. Specify a case in which $Fb \land Ga$, $\neg \exists x Fx$, and $\neg \exists x Gx$ are all true.

3. Specify which of the following are valid arguments, and justify your answer.

   (a) $\forall x Fx \therefore Fa$

   (b) $Fb \land Gb \therefore \exists x (Fx \land Gx)$

---

[8]Here (and below), we're using '$\therefore$' just to separate premises from conclusion.

    (c) $\neg \exists x F x \therefore \neg F b$

    (d) $\neg F a \therefore \neg \forall x F x$

4. If only the objects in E exist in a given case, but $E \subseteq D$ (for any case), what is the 'ontological status' of elements in $\{x : x \in D \text{ and } x \notin E\}$, the so-called complement of E relative to D. (The complement of E relative to D is often denoted by either '$D \setminus E$' or '$D - E$')?

5. If 'Guy Stewart' really doesn't denote *anything*, then 'Guy Stewart' doesn't denote anything—full stop. So, if 'Guy Stewart' doesn't denote anything, then it doesn't denote anything in the 'big domain' D. What, if anything, does this suggest about our formal modeling of the matter?

6. You might reject that there are predicates that are true of objects that don't exist. (E.g., you might reject that 'Agnes is thinking about x' is true of the *so-called object* Guy.) Instead of drawing the lesson that some of our predicates can be true of objects that don't exist, what other lessons might you draw from the Guy Stewart story?

7. We have said (in this and previous chapters) that existence claims like *b exists* have the form $\exists x(x = b)$. You might be wondering about a different approach: treating 'exists' as a more standard, quantifier-free predicate. How might this go? Is the predicate to be treated as a logical expression? If so, what are the constraints on its extension and antiextension? If the predicate is non-logical (i.e., its extension and antiextension get no special constraints aside from those imposed on all predicates by the kind of cases involved), how do existence claims like *b exists* relate to existential claims like $\exists x(x = b)$? What, in general, is the logic of your proposed existence predicate? (This question is left wide open as an opportunity for you to construct your own alternative logical theory of existence.)

Sample answers

Answer 3a. The argument from $\forall x F x$ to $F a$ is not valid (according to the current freed up theory). To see this, let c be any of our (current, freed-up) cases in which $\delta(a) \notin E$ (i.e., in which the denotation of name a is not among the objects that, according to c, exist), and let $\delta(a) \notin F^+$ (i.e., the denotation of a is not in the set of objects that, according to c, have the property F), and let everything else in D be in the extension of F (i.e., be in F^+). This case is a counterexample to the given argument.

11

Possibilities

Es gibt viele Möglichkeiten,
aber nicht mehr als die Notwendigkeit erlaubt.
(There are many possibilities,
but not more than necessity permits.)
– Hair Rossberg

In this chapter we briefly explore a few so-called modal connectives: possibility and necessity. To accommodate the notions of necessity and possibility, we add new connectives to the syntax of our language and, in turn, modify our account of cases.

11.1 Possibility and necessity

Imagine being a world maker. Imagine that you were in charge of creating a world. What would your world be like? Would you make the world just like this one—just like the actual world (the way things actually are)? Would you make it have cats? Would there be rocks and trees in your world? What about pain? What about religion? What about politicians, lawyers, and the like? Would your world contain thinking beings?

Presumably, there are lots of options for your creation: there are many ways that you could make your world. On the other hand, your options aren't without constraints: you can't do the impossible; you can't transgress what's necessary. If, for example, it's necessary that circles are right-angle-free, then you can't make your world have right-angled circles. Similarly, if it's necessary that Max is identical to Max, then you can't make a world in which Max is not Max. Of course, so long as Max is not a necessary entity—an entity that must exist—you can make a world in which Max doesn't exist; however, you can't make a world in which Max is not Max.

The broad notion of possibility at work in our imagined world-making exercise is sometimes called 'broadly logical possibility', or 'logical possibility', or the like. (The terminology, regrettably, is neither uniform nor precise.) We shall simply use 'possibility'. Possibility, in this sense, is about as unconstrained as one can get; it is constrained only by the limits of logical coherence. As such, one might think of the target operator along the lines of *it is logically coherent that*, and the corresponding necessity operator as *it is logically mandatory* or the like. In this respect, what is possible (or, correspondingly, necessary) is controversial. If the classical logical theory is in force, then it's impossible for sentences of the form $A \wedge \neg A$ to be true or, similarly, for $A \vee \neg A$ to be untrue. Paracomplete and paraconsistent theories recognize more logical options, and so acknowledge a broader space of logical coherence—a broader space of possibilities.

For present purposes, we shall set aside the controversial issue of possibility's limits (i.e., of the limits of our target notion of possibility). We shall leave the informal notion rather loose and vague: we leave the limits of possibility to the limits of your world-making. If, for your world-making work, there's a candidate world at which A is true (i.e., if you can make a world at which A is true), then A is possible. If not, then A is impossible. And if *every* candidate world is one at which A is true, then A is necessary (i.e., necessarily true).

The target connectives *it is possible that* and *it is necessary that* are sometimes called *modal* connectives—or, more fully, *alethic* (from the Greek word for truth) modal connectives— because they specify a 'mode' or 'way' in which claims are true (e.g., necessarily true, or possibly true, etc.). In what follows, we briefly discuss a standard account of the given modal connectives, beginning with the issue of truth conditions.

11.2   Towards truth and falsity conditions

Following standard practice, we shall introduce two new connectives: $\diamond$ shall be our *it is possible that* connective, and $\square$ shall be our corresponding necessity connective (viz., *it is necessary that*). The question at hand is: what are the truth and falsity conditions for these connectives?

11.2.1 *Truth at a world*

In previous chapters, we've looked at truth-in-a-case conditions for various connectives. We still want to do that, but our new modal connectives involve a prior condition: *truth at a world*. The idea, going back to the mathematician and philosopher Leibniz, is fairly intuitive.

Think of reality as a universe of 'worlds'. Whatever else they are, worlds are things at which sentences can be true or false. Worlds, then, may be 'complete' in the sense that, for every sentence A, either A or its negation $\neg A$ is true at the world.[1] Similarly, worlds may be 'consistent' in the sense that, for every sentence A, not both A and $\neg A$ are true at the world. (A classical conception of worlds has it that they're one and all complete and consistent in the given sense.) But, of course, it may be that some worlds are incomplete, some inconsistent, and some both incomplete and inconsistent.[2]

In many respects, then, worlds are like the 'cases' encountered in previous chapters. But our *cases*, now, are more like the 'universes' that house our worlds. Instead of talking simply of *truth in a case*, we now shall talk of *truth at a world in a case*—or, more flowery, *truth at a world in a universe*.[3] So, our *truth at* relation now has an extra slot: instead of writing

$$c \models_1 A$$

we now write

$$[c, w] \models_1 A$$

---

[1] A note on notation: to avoid too much hyphenation, I drop hyphens from 'true-at-a-world' and, similarly, from 'true-at-a-world-in-a-case' (and the like).

[2] I should note that some philosophers reserve the word 'worlds' (in this sort of context) for complete and consistent worlds; any 'world' that's either incomplete or inconsistent is thought to be something other than a proper world—perhaps a 'situation' or some such item (Barwise and Perry, 1983; Barwise, 1989). For present purposes, 'world' remains neutral on matters of completeness and consistency.

[3] Lest some be allergic to flowers, such talk can be put in a colorless package: truth at a *point* in a *model*. But color, as my mother used to say, makes the world go around.

where w is a world in the given universe c. Similarly, we write $[c, w] \models_0 A$ for A *is false at w in c*. For convenience, we often leave reference to a given case implicit, writing $w \models_1 A$ and $w \models_0 A$.

11.2.2   *Truth at a world (in a universe): atomics*

We assume, as suggested above, that every universe/case c comes equipped with a set $\mathcal{W}$ of worlds. In addition, we assume that every such universe contains a domain D, namely, the set of all objects whatsoever—the set of all objects that, according to the given case (universe), one can talk about. Moreover, towards 'freedom of speech' (see Chapter 10), we assume that, for any universe (case), every world w in the given universe comes equipped with a *world-relative-existence domain* E_w, where E_w is a subset of D comprising all objects that, according to the given case (or universe), exist at w. (This existence set, as in previous chapters, is relevant only when we get to the quantifiers; however, it's useful to note it here in combination with D.)

What we need to do is first give *truth at a world (in a universe)* conditions for our atomics and, in turn, molecular sentences—including the new modal sentences.

Atomics. Recall that, in previous chapters, what matters for the truth (falsity) of atomics are the extensions (antiextensions) of predicates and denotations of terms. The question, then, is how these things work in our world-involving framework.

For our purposes, *denotation* remains exactly as before: our denotation function δ assigns an object $\delta(\alpha)$ from the domain D to each name α.[4] In this respect, our names are so-called rigid designators: they denote the same object at all worlds—regardless of whether the object exists at the world, that is, regardless of the object's status in E_w.[5]

---

[4] We also assume, as throughout, that each element of the domain has a name.

[5] Kripke (1972) coined the term 'rigid designator' for this kind of behavior: denoting the same object at all worlds (at which the the object exists). Can you think of an alternative account of how our names might work—and how your alternative might affect truth (falsity) conditions for atomics? (We won't go into alternatives here, but the topic rewards reflection.)

Extensions/antiextensions. In the current world-involving framework, extensions and antiextensions of predicates likewise remain as before (e.g., Chapters 8–10), except that we now relativize things to worlds. Consider, for example, the predicate 'has black hair'. Agnes actually has black hair, but she could've had red hair or blond hair or even no hair at all. (Imagine your world-making exercise, and your selection of a world in which Agnes has red instead of black hair.) So, Agnes is in the extension of 'has black hair' at some worlds, but not in the extension of 'has black hair' at other worlds. What this suggests is that the extensions of our predicates vary from world to world. Another example, of course, is 'exists'. Unless Agnes necessarily exists—that is, exists at all worlds whatsoever—then Agnes fails to exist at some worlds (and, so, fails to be in the extension of 'exists' at some worlds). We assume, then, that for each world w, each predicate Π has an extension and antiextension at w. Intuitively, the extension of Π at w comprises all objects of which Π is true, and the antiextension all objects of which Π is false.

With the foregoing ingredients in hand, our world-relative truth (falsity) conditions for atomics are as you'd expect.

- An atomic $\Pi\alpha_1, \ldots, \alpha_n$ is true at a world w in universe c if and only if $\langle \delta(\alpha_1), \ldots, \delta(\alpha_n) \rangle$ is in Π's extension at w.
- An atomic $\Pi\alpha_1, \ldots, \alpha_n$ is false at a world w in universe c if and only if $\langle \delta(\alpha_1), \ldots, \delta(\alpha_n) \rangle$ is in Π's antiextension at w.

Our *logical identity predicate* is treated exactly as in previous chapters, except now relativized to worlds.

- For any case c, the extension of '$=$' at a world w is the set of all (and only) 'identity pairs' $\langle \delta(\alpha), \delta(\alpha) \rangle$ for each object $\delta(\alpha)$ in c's domain.
- For any case c, the antiextension of '$=$' at a world w is any set of pairs $\langle \delta(\alpha_i), \delta(\alpha_j) \rangle$ for any objects $\delta(\alpha_i)$ and $\delta(\alpha_j)$ in c's domain.

So, except for the relativity to worlds, truth (falsity) conditions for all atomics remain as before.[6]

---

[6]One can tighten (and increase plausibility of?) one's logical theory of identity via more restrictions on the antiextension (e.g., requiring that it contain all *non-identity pairs* or some variation on this).

11.2.3   *Truth at a world (in a universe): molecular*

With the above conditions for atomics, we can now give truth (falsity) conditions for molecular sentences. We break this up into the non-modal (in effect, the connectives covered in previous chapters) and our new modal connectives.

11.2.3.1   *Basic connectives and quantifiers.*   Conditions for our basic connectives are as you would expect, now relativized to worlds.

- $A \wedge B$ is true at w in c iff A and B are true at w in c.
- $A \wedge B$ is false at w in c iff A or B is false at w in c.

- $A \vee B$ is true at w in c iff A or B is true at w in c.
- $A \vee B$ is false at w in c iff A and B are false at w in c.

- $\neg A$ is true at w in c iff A is false at w in c.
- $\neg A$ is false at w in c iff A is true at w in c.

Clauses for the quantifiers are 'freed up' as per Chapter 10, except now relativized to worlds via the world-relative existence domain E_w.[7] For convenience, we call any object in E_w an E_w *object*.

- $\exists v(\ldots v \ldots)$ is true at w in c iff $\ldots v \ldots$ is true of some E_w object.

- $\exists v(\ldots v \ldots)$ is false at w in c iff $\ldots v \ldots$ is false of every E_w object.

- $\forall v(\ldots v \ldots)$ is true at w in c iff $\ldots v \ldots$ is true of every E_w object.

- $\forall v(\ldots v \ldots)$ is false at w in c iff $\ldots v \ldots$ is false of some E_w object.

So, again, all remains much as before except for the relativization to worlds.

---

[7]Note that, once again (see Chapter 9), we're very loosely using talk of a 'condition' $\ldots v \ldots$ being 'true of' and/or 'false of' objects. We haven't (and, for simplicity, won't) define this; and in fact we use a so-called substitutional approach to truth conditions in our formal picture. (If one wants, one can define an E_w *name* (relative to a given case or universe) to be a name α such that $\delta(\alpha) \in E_w$. If one does this, then we can rewrite the informal truth conditions invoking an E_w-*name instance* of $\ldots v \ldots$. But these sorts of detail are left for other, more rigorous, exhaustive introductions to logical theory.)

11.2.3.2   *Modal connectives: possibility and necessity.*   The big question concerns our new connectives: our modal connectives for possibility and necessity, namely, $\Diamond$ and $\Box$. Here, the picture mentioned above is telling: each world in a universe represents— or just is—a possibility. So, for a possibility claim $\Diamond A$ to be true at a world w (in universe c, etc.) is for there to be some world w' (not necessarily distinct from w) at which A is true.

- $\Diamond A$ is true at w in c iff A is true at some w' in c.
- $\Diamond A$ is false at w in c iff A is false at all w' in c.

Similarly, since necessity amounts to truth at all possibilities, $\Box A$ is true at a world w just if A is true at *all* worlds w' in the universe.

- $\Box A$ is true at w in c iff A is true at all w' in c.
- $\Box A$ is false at w in c iff A is false at some w' in c.

11.3   Cases and consequence

Logical consequence, as throughout this book, is absence of counterexample, absence of any case in which the premises are true but conclusion untrue. Our cases are now 'universes' along the foregoing lines. The question, though, concerns *truth in a case* or *truth in a universe*. So far, we've specified what it is for sentences to be *true at worlds in universes*, but we have yet to say what it is for a sentence to be true-in-a-case/universe simpliciter. We address that question here, and then turn to a swift, hopefully slightly clearer account of everything in the 'formal picture' in §11.4.

11.3.1   *Actuality and truth in a case*

The question is: how is *truth in a case* to be defined? As it turns out, there are various (equivalent) options. For present purposes, we shall take a very intuitive approach. In particular, we shall say that, in addition to its other worlds in $\mathcal{W}$, each universe c comes equipped with a special, so-called *actual* world @. (Intuitively, we live in the actual world, which is one of many possible worlds in our actual universe.) And it's in terms of this special world, within each universe, that we define *truth in a case*.

- We say that A is true-in-a-universe (case) c if and only if A is true at c's actual world, that is, if and only if $[c, @] \models_1 A$.

Similarly, we define *falsity in a case/universe* in terms of the actual world of the given universe.

- We say that A is false-in-a-universe (case) c if and only if A is false at c's actual world, that is, if and only if $[c, @] \models_0 A$.

For clarity, we say that A is *untrue–in-a-case-c* (similarly, not true-in-c) just if A does not stand in c's truth relation to @, that is, just if $[c, @] \not\models_1 A$. As in previous chapters, without further constraints on cases, we can have sentences that are untrue-in-a-case without those sentences being false-in-a-case; and we can have sentences that are false-in-a-case without their being untrue-in-the-case. (If you don't see this, be sure to think back to previous FDE-related distinctions, and look again at the few constraints governing our cases in this chapter. There are exercises along these lines.)

11.3.2   *Consequence*

To have a handy name, let us use 'Mfde' for the logical theory falling out of the present account of necessity and possibility. (The 'M' is for 'modal', and the 'fde' is as before except lowercase—in effect, our glutty–gappy theory, extended with quantifiers and, now, modal connectives.) A clearer account of the *cases* recognized by this theory (Mfde) is given in the formal picture (see §11.4).

And now, finally, we define our core notion *Mfde consequence* as you'd expect: absence of counterexample. In other words: B is an Mfde consequence of A if and only if there's no Mfde case (universe) in which A is true but B untrue.

What are some of the properties of possibility and necessity delivered by this account? This question is addressed by some of the exercises at the end of the chapter. For now, we turn to a slightly more formal sketch of the foregoing ideas.

11.4   Formal picture

The formal picture is only a slight variation on the above, and largely overlaps with that of Chapter 10, and so we can be brief.

11.4.1   *Syntax*

The syntax is exactly that of Chapter 9 except for two additional logical expressions: $\Diamond$ and $\Box$ are added as unary connectives. Accordingly, the definition of *sentences* is as before, except that now we add another clause covering our new molecular (and, in this case, modal) sentences.

- If A is a sentence of the language, so too are $\Diamond A$ and $\Box A$.

11.4.2   *Semantics*

The semantic picture, as discussed above, is much as before, except for adding worlds into the picture. Our cases are now structures $\langle \mathcal{W}, @, D, \mathcal{E}_w, \delta \rangle$, where $@$, the so-called actual world of the universe/case, is in $\mathcal{W}$, a non-empty set comprising all worlds of the given case. $D \neq \emptyset$ and, as before, is the domain of all objects recognized by the given case. $\mathcal{E}_w$, in turn, is a set of *world-relative existence sets* E_w, each of which is a subset of D and houses the 'existing objects' in the given case. (Note that an existence set E_w, unlike D, can be empty, in which case nothing exists at w.) The role of δ is exactly as in previous chapters, except that it assigns world-relative extensions and antiextensions to predicates. In particular, with respect to names, δ assigns an object $\delta(\alpha)$ from D to each name α. With respect to predicates, δ takes every world w and predicate Π and assigns pair $\langle \Pi_w^+, \Pi_w^- \rangle$, where Π_w^+ and Π_w^- are the extension and, respectively, antiextension of Π at w. Note that, as in earlier chapters, Π_w^+ and Π_w^- are subsets of D^n. (As in Chapter 10, we do not demand that extensions and extensions be drawn from the given existence set E_w.)

With all of this in mind, the full truth (falsity) conditions are given as follows, where, as in previous chapters, α is any name, and we assume that everything in the domain (of any case) has a name α_i in the language, and $A(\alpha/\mathsf{v})$ is the result of replacing all (free) occurrences of v in A with the name α.

« *Note well.* Because we are treating the extension and antiextension of identity (viz., $\mathcal{E}_{=}^+$ and $\mathcal{E}_{=}^-$) uniformly across all worlds—the (anti-) extension is the same at all worlds—we drop the reference to worlds in the following semantic clauses for identity (thereby keeping the clause the same as in previous chapters). We also use 'st' as an abbreviation for 'such that' (a space-saver). *End note.* »

- Atomics
  - ∗ General
    $[c, w] \models_1 \Pi\alpha_1, \ldots, \alpha_n$ iff $\langle \delta(\alpha_1), \ldots, \delta(\alpha_n) \rangle \in \Pi_w^+$.
    $[c, w] \models_0 \Pi\alpha_1, \ldots, \alpha_n$ iff $\langle \delta(\alpha_1), \ldots, \delta(\alpha_n) \rangle \in \Pi_w^-$.
  - ∗ Logical (viz., Identity)
    $\mathcal{E}_=^+ = \{\langle \delta(\alpha), \delta(\alpha) \rangle : \delta(\alpha) \in D\}$.
    $\mathcal{E}_=^- \subseteq D \times D$.
- Basic connectives
  $[c, w] \models_1 \neg A$ iff $[c, w] \models_0 A$.
  $[c, w] \models_0 \neg A$ iff $[c, w] \models_1 A$.

  $[c, w] \models_1 A \vee B$ iff $[c, w] \models_1 A$ or $[c, w] \models_1 B$.
  $[c, w] \models_0 A \vee B$ iff $[c, w] \models_0 A$ and $[c, w] \models_0 B$.

  $[c, w] \models_1 A \wedge B$ iff $[c, w] \models_1 A$ and $[c, w] \models_1 B$.
  $[c, w] \models_0 A \wedge B$ iff $[c, w] \models_0 A$ or $[c, w] \models_0 B$.
- Quantifiers
  $[c, w] \models_1 \exists \mathsf{v} A$ iff $[c, w] \models_1 A(\alpha/\mathsf{v})$ for some α st $\delta(\alpha) \in E_w$.
  $[c, w] \models_0 \exists \mathsf{v} A$ iff $[c, w] \models_0 A(\alpha/\mathsf{v})$ for all α st $\delta(\alpha) \in E_w$.

  $[c, w] \models_1 \forall \mathsf{v} A$ iff $[c, w] \models_1 A(\alpha/\mathsf{v})$ for all α st $\delta(\alpha) \in E_w$.
  $[c, w] \models_0 \forall \mathsf{v} A$ iff $[c, w] \models_0 A(\alpha/\mathsf{v})$ for some α st $\delta(\alpha) \in E_w$.
- Modal connectives
  $[c, w] \models_1 \Diamond A$ iff there's some $w' \in \mathcal{W}$ st $[c, w'] \models_1 A$.
  $[c, w] \models_0 \Diamond A$ iff every $w' \in \mathcal{W}$ is st $[c, w'] \models_0 A$.

  $[c, w] \models_1 \Box A$ iff every $w' \in \mathcal{W}$ is st $[c, w'] \models_1 A$.
  $[c, w] \models_0 \Box A$ iff there's some $w' \in \mathcal{W}$ st $[c, w'] \models_0 A$.

Truth in a case (similarly, falsity in a case) is defined in terms of the actual world of the case: A is true-in-c iff $[c, @] \models_1 A$, and similarly false-in-c iff $[c, @] \models_0 A$.

We now define *consequence* as we have throughout: absence of counterexample, where a counterexample is now any such Mfde case in which the premises are true and conclusion untrue.

11.4.3   *A few notable forms*

Our Mfde account, as some of the exercises indicate, delivers the validity of standard argument forms involving alethic possibility and necessity operators—our *it is logically coherent that* and *it is logically mandatory that* operators. To illustrate the main ones, let us use the following terminology for any operator or unary connective Ω (pronounced *Omega*, the last letter of the Greek alphabet.)

- Capture: Ω *captures* iff A implies ΩA for all sentences A.
- Release: Ω *releases* iff ΩA implies A for all sentences A.[8]

With this terminology in hand, note that the Mfde account of $\Box$ and $\Diamond$ has it that $\Diamond$ *captures but does not release* while $\Box$ *releases but does not capture*. In particular, where $\vdash$ is our given Mfde consequence relation, we have the following.

$$A \vdash \Diamond A$$

To see this (viz., that $\Diamond$ captures), simply notice that there cannot be an Mfde case in which A is true but $\Diamond A$ not true. After all, if, for some such case c, we have $[c, @] \models_1 A$, then the truth condition for $\Diamond A$ immediately delivers $[c, @] \models_1 \Diamond A$ since there's a world—viz., @ itself—at which A is true. Since this applies to any (arbitrary) case c, we conclude that there cannot be a counterexample to the form $A \therefore \Diamond A$ (i.e., $\Diamond$ Capture).

On the other hand, $\Diamond$ does not release:

$$\Diamond A \nvdash A$$

That this is so is revealed by a counterexample. For simplicity, let A be a simple atomic like Fb. Consider a two-world case c in which $\mathcal{W} = \{@, w\}$ and $D = \{1\}$ and $\delta(b) = 1$ and $F_@^+ = \emptyset$ and $F_w^+ = \{1\}$.[9] A careful look at the truth conditions (for atomics and diamond claims) shows that, since there's at least one world in the given universe/case (viz., w) such that $[c, w] \models_1 Fb$, we have it that $[c, @] \models_1 \Diamond Fb$. But since $\delta(b) \notin F_@^+$, we have $[c, @] \nvDash_1 Fb$.

---

[8]Some philosophers use the term *factive* instead of *release*, saying that Ω is 'factive' iff ΩA implies A for all sentences A. The reason behind the 'factive' terminology arises from the thought that 'it is a fact that' is itself an operator (or connective) that releases. (In this respect, the 'release' terminology is more general.)

[9]Note that one can let $E_@$ and E_w be whatever one likes, and similarly let the antiextension of F at @ and w be whatever one likes; none of this affects the current countermodel. (Why?)

Hence, this is a case in which $\Diamond A$ is true but A not true (where A is Fb). Hence, the given argument form (viz., $\Diamond$ Release) fails in Mfde.

This is all as we should want. Regardless of whether Agnes is actually sleeping, if it's true that Agnes is sleeping, then it's logically coherent that Agnes is sleeping. More abstractly: if A is true, then it's logically coherent that A is true. This is simply Capture for our given 'possibility' operator. On the other hand, that it's logically coherent that Agnes is sleeping hardly implies that Agnes is sleeping! There are lots of logically coherent things that never get a taste of actuality (so to speak). Example: it's logically coherent that—despite appearances—you are not really reading a book right now but only seem to be doing so. (You might, as Rene Descartes feared, be in the grips of an evil demon who is making it seem like you're reading a book even though you're not.) But—as you well know (contrary to Descartes and his demon!)—you are reading a book right now. So, our 'possibility' operator does not release.

Similar (in fact, so-called dual) considerations establish that, as mentioned above, our *it is logically mandatory that* operator (i.e., our 'necessity' operator) *releases* but *does not capture*. In other words, we have $\Box A \vdash A$ but $A \nvdash \Box A$ according to our Mfde theory. That this is so is left as an exercise.

11.5   Remark on going beyond possibility

You might think, as many logicians do, that other common connectives should be handled along similar truth-at-a-world lines. Consider one prominent example: *it is morally obligatory that*. When reading the box as this connective, surely A does not follow from $\Box A$. After all, it's morally obligatory that nobody be murdered; however, murder happens. So, the logic of 'it is morally obligatory that' is different from 'it is necessarily true that'. In short: the latter releases while the former does not. (Like 'necessity', the moral-obligation connective does not capture. You are reading this sentence, but it's not morally obligatory that you do so!) The question is whether the same sort of truth-at-a-world semantics can be given for the former connective.

The answer shared by many is affirmative. What we want to do, however, is constrain the worlds we look at in our truth (falsity) conditions for the box (now read in the moral-obligation sense). We don't want to look at *all* worlds; we want to look only at all *relevant* ones. In the case of moral connectives—the truth conditions for (say) *it is morally obligatory that*—we want to look only at the 'morally relevant worlds', the worlds where the moral laws, whatever they are, are obeyed. (Here, for simplicity, we can think of the set of moral laws as being fixed across our universe of all worlds. A world in the universe obeys the moral laws iff all laws in the set of moral laws are true at the world.) If we think of the *logical coherence* reading of the box (i.e., $\Box$) as talking about all worlds where the 'laws of logical coherence' (or, if you want, 'logical laws') hold, then we can think of the *morally obligatory* reading along analogous lines: it talks about all worlds where the moral laws are obeyed.

« *Parenthetical remark.* I noted above that, for simplicity, we simply think of the set of moral laws being fixed across the universe. For our present (very limited) purposes, this will do (and is what we shall do below); however, there's an alternative way of looking at what's going on, a very world-relativistic angle of sorts. In particular, we can imagine that each world comes equipped with a moral-law book (perhaps written by some Moral Authority), a book that specifies what, *according to that world*, count as the moral laws. The *morally relevant worlds*, according to a given world w, are all the worlds that obey w's moral-law book (i.e., all of the worlds at which all of w's moral-law book's claims are true). On this way of looking at matters, the morally relevant worlds can differ from world to world. (A world w's moral-law book may be true only of worlds $w_1, w_2, \ldots, w_5$, while another world's moral-law book may be true of w_6 but none of $w_1, w_2, \ldots, w_5$.) For present purposes, whether you think of 'morally relevant worlds' along this explicitly relativistic line or along the fixed-across-all-worlds fashion will not matter. (As an exercise, you might consider whether there's a difference that could make a difference to the logic of the moral-obligation operator.) *End parenthetical.* »

To make formal sense of this, we simply expand our account of cases (our universes) to have a binary relation R on $\mathcal{W}$, so that our cases now look like $\langle \mathcal{W}, R, D, \mathcal{E}_w, \delta \rangle$. In effect, R tells you what worlds are relevant to what worlds. For necessity and possibility, we let R be reflexive, symmetric, and transitive. (For a reminder on what this amounts to, see §3.3.1.) For our *moral* connective at hand, we want to avoid release; we don't want A following from $\Box A$. One way of doing this is to let R be unconstrained in our account of cases, and to make a minor modification to the truth conditions at work in the logic of 'necessity'. In particular, we say that our 'moral cases' are structures $\langle \mathcal{W}, R, D, \mathcal{E}_w, \delta \rangle$ where R may be any binary relation on $\mathcal{W}$ (and, so, R doesn't have to be reflexive, etc.). In turn, instead of saying that $\Box A$ (now informally read as 'it is morally obligatory that A') is true at a world w iff A is true at *all* w', we say instead that $\Box A$ is true at w iff A is true at all *(morally) relevant* (or, as it's sometimes put, *accessible*) w'. In other words, we adjust the formal truth conditions for the box as follows—where, *note very well*, w' is a *w-accessible world* if and only if wRw'.[10]

$[c, w] \models_1 \Box A$ iff every w-accessible world is st $[c, w'] \models_1 A$.

$[c, w] \models_0 \Box A$ iff there's some w-accessible world st $[c, w'] \models_0 A$.

How does this adjustment help? Well, consider a case c in which @ is not morally relevant, not morally obedient—a case such that $\langle @, @ \rangle \notin R$. One might think of this as a case in which the moral laws—which, for simplicity, we're supposing to be the same throughout the universe—are not obeyed at @.

« *Parenthetical remark.* On the openly world-relative account of moral laws mentioned above—invoking a world's moral-law book—one can think of the case c at hand as one where @ is not morally relevant to itself, that is, a case in which @'s moral-law book is not obeyed by @.) *End parenthetical.* »

However one thinks of it, the case provides what we need for a counterexample to $\Box$-Release (where, again, $\Box$ is now thought of along moral-obligation lines). In particular, ignoring the details of our sentence A, suppose that $\mathcal{W} = \{ @, w \}$, and that A is true at

---

[10] As in previous chapters, 'st' is sometimes used as a space-saving shorthand for 'such that'.

w but not at @.[11] Moreover, suppose that w is morally relevant to @, that is, that w is an @-accessible (morally obedient) world in our given universe—that is, that we have @Rw in the given case (though not, as said, @R@). Well, then, since the only worlds are @ and w, it's clear that every @-accessible world (viz., w) in the given universe is one at which A is true. Hence, $\Box A$ is true at @. But we have it that A is not true at @. Hence, we have a case in which $\Box A$ but not A is true. Hence, as we wanted (at least on the moral-obligation reading), $\Box$-Release fails in this setup.

In addition to the moral-obligation and logical-coherence connectives, there are many other connectives in natural language that appear to be box-like (so to speak). For present purposes, these are left to your reflection (but some are suggested in exercises too).

Summary and looking ahead

Summary. In this chapter we have briefly explored a few basic modal notions: broad possibility and broad necessity. We've treated these notions (exactly along standard lines) as, in effect, quantifiers over possible worlds. To model this idea, we've expanded our 'cases' with a set of worlds, each world representing what, according to the case, is a possibility (in the target broad sense). A *necessity claim* $\Box A$ is true at a world iff A is true at *all* worlds, and a *possiblity claim* $\Diamond A$ is true at a world iff A is true at *some* world. Each such case—or universe (in which a bunch of worlds reside)—comes equipped with an actual world @ in terms of which *truth in a case* (similarly for *falsity*) is defined. Consequence, in turn, is then defined via the guiding recipe from Chapter 1: absence of a case (universe) in which all premises are true but conclusion untrue. In order to get logics of different (modal) connectives (e.g., *it is morally obligatory that...*, among other connectives), we can invoke an 'accessibility relation' on our universe of worlds: a relation that picks out a subset of our universe, namely, the set of *relevant worlds* (worlds relevant to the 'nature' of the connective at hand).

---

[11] Strictly speaking, the additional world w is unnecessary for the counterexample, but it avoids a detour explaining the 'vacuous' sense in which all box claims are true at w if there are no w-accessible worlds.

Looking Ahead. If you've made it this far in the book, you might as well go one more chapter. In the next and final chapter, we very quickly march through a few variations on themes from previous chapters, looking at (alas, only a very few) different avenues for further logical exploration.

Further Reading. Among the accessible and related discussions of modal logics are Hughes and Cresswell 1996, Chellas 1980, and Girle 2000. More directly related to the non-classical logical theories are textbooks mentioned in previous chapters, namely, Beall and van Fraassen 2003; Priest 2008; Restall 2005. (Of course, many more sources may be found via the bibliographies of all such books.) For an accessible history of contemporary possible-worlds semantics, see Copeland 2002, which gives a broad bibliography of key sources, and also (for specifically so-called Priorean modal logic) see the much more advanced Menzel 1991.

Exercises

Unless otherwise stated, the Mfde truth conditions (see §11.4.2) are assumed in the following exercises.

1. Which of the following arguments are valid? Justify your answer (with a proof or counterexample).[12]
   (a) $\Box(Fb \wedge Fa) \therefore \Box Fb \wedge \Box Fa$
   (b) $\Box Fb \therefore \Diamond Fb$
   (c) $\Diamond Fb \therefore \Box Fb$
   (d) $\Box(a = a) \therefore \Diamond \exists x(x = a)$
   (e) $\Box \neg \exists x(x = a) \therefore \neg(a = a)$
   (f) $\Box \Diamond Fa \therefore \Diamond \Box Fa$
   (g) $\neg \Diamond \exists x(x = a) \therefore \neg \Box(a = a)$

2. Are there cases in which $a = a$ is not true? If so, provide one. If not, show as much.

3. Are there cases in which $\Box(a = a)$ is not true? If so, provide one. If not, show as much.

4. Is $\Diamond(a = a)$ logically true?

---

[12]Here, we use '$\therefore$' merely to separate premises and conclusion. (The following are arguments from our formal language, not argument forms.)

5. Explain how to modify Mfde to get the following results (i.e., for the resulting, modified consequence relation). If no modification is required for a given item, prove as much.

   (a) $\Box A \wedge \Box \neg A \vdash B$

   (b) $\vdash \Box A \vee \neg \Box A$

   (c) $\vdash \Box (A \vee \neg A)$

   (d) $\Box A, \Diamond \neg A \vdash B$

   (e) $\vdash \forall x \Diamond \exists y (y = x)$

6. Suppose that we define a world w (of a case c) to be *consistent* iff there's no sentence A such that $[c, w] \models_1 A$ and $[c, w] \models_0 A$. Similarly, suppose that we define a world w (of a case c) to be *complete* iff there's no sentence A such that $[c, w] \not\models_1 A$ and $[c, w] \not\models_0 A$ (i.e., the world is such that every sentence is either true at the world or false at the world). Precisely formulate and explore the following, narrower (though stronger) variations on Mfde.

   (a) K3 Modal: the cases are all Mfde cases *that contain only consistent worlds* (though not necessarily complete).

   (b) LP Modal: the cases are all Mfde cases *that contain only complete worlds* (though not necessarily consistent).

   (c) Classical (though 'free') Modal: the cases are all Mfde cases *that contain only consistent and complete worlds*.[13]

   For each of the resulting logics in (6a)–(6c), go through all questions from Exercises 1–5 again but focus on the given narrower logic.

7. What other connectives might be treated along 'worlds' lines? What if, instead of thinking of the elements in $\mathcal{W}$ as *worlds*, we think of $\mathcal{W}$ as containing *points in time*. Now consider the connectives *it is always true that...* and *it is sometimes true that....* If we treat these connectives along our box and, respectively, diamond lines, what sort of 'temporal logic' (i.e., logic of such temporal connectives) do we get? Related question: what sort of 'ordering' on your points

---

[13]The freedom comes from our speaking-freely approach to cases. See Chapter 10.

in $\mathcal{W}$ do you need to give in order to add plausible *it will be true that...* and *it was true that...* connectives into the picture? (E.g., do your points of time have to be ordered in the way that, e.g., the natural numbers are ordered?)

Sample answers

Answer 4. Yes, $\Diamond(a = a)$ is logically true. Suppose, for reductio, that it is not logically true, in which case there must be a case (universe) in which $\Diamond(a = a)$ is untrue, that is, a case c such that $[c, @] \not\models_1 \Diamond(a = a)$. But, then, by the truth conditions for the diamond, there must be no world in our given case (universe) at which $a = a$ is true. But by the constraints on identity (viz., that the extension of the identity predicate contains *all* pairs of objects from the domain of the given case), $a = a$ is true at all worlds. Hence, we've run into an unacceptable contradiction (viz., that there is both some world in our case and no world in our case in which $a = a$ is true), and so we reject our initial supposition that $\Diamond(a = a)$ is not logically true. We conclude, then, that $\Diamond(a = a)$ is logically true.

12

Glimpsing Different Logical Roads

> *Two roads diverged in a wood, and I –*
> *I took the one less traveled by,*
> *And that has made all the difference.*
> – Robert Frost
> 'The Road Not Taken'

In the previous chapters you've explored a sample of logical theories. All of the theories so far discussed are in broad agreement not only on the set of logical expressions (i.e., on what should be counted among our logical expressions), but also *roughly* on how they should be treated—on what the truth-in-a-case conditions are for the given expressions. (The differences among the theories discussed so far are largely differences on what sort of cases should be acknowledged, but not on how truth-in-a-case is to be defined for the various expressions.)

There are many more logical theories than mentioned—let alone discussed—in this book. One route towards difference involves recognizing more (or, for that matter, fewer) connectives than we have so far discussed. Another route towards difference retains the same set of logical expressions but, for various philosophical (or other) reasons, treats the logical expressions—that is, their truth (or truth-in-a-case) conditions—differently.

In this chapter, we briefly glance along a few such roads towards different logical theories—theories that either expand the logical theories of previous chapters or downright conflict with them. The aim is not so much to present details of particular theories, but rather to wave in a few directions towards which rival, or at least different, logical theories may emerge. Due to space, only a very, very few such 'logical roads' are waved at, and so the 'further reading' section is particularly important at this stage.

The chapter proceeds via a rapid march through various—not necessarily connected—phenomena that motivate logical theories that go beyond or differ from theories of the previous chapters. You should think of other phenomena that motivate logical exploration! There are many more phenomena that bear on logical theory than are mentioned in this book.

12.1   Other conditionals

One of the most fruitful areas for logical theorizing concerns conditionals. Notice, for example, that the conditional we've used throughout Chapters 1–11 (viz., the so-called *material conditional*) is true so long as the antecedent is false or the consequent true. Hence, 'if Barack Obama is 3-feet tall, then *Logic: The Basics* is everyone's favorite book' is true when the 'if' is treated along material-conditional lines. (The antecedent is false. I take no stand on the consequent!) While the material-conditional account may be true of some conditional—or some (conditional) usage of *if*—in our language, it seems not to be true of all. There also seem to be other conditionals—or (conditional) uses of *if*— that require a stronger connection between antecedent and consequent.

There are many (many) different routes towards adding other conditionals to the language. (See *further reading*.) But before one goes about adding a new connective and giving it truth/falsity conditions, one should pause to consider whether the current language already has something that will do the trick. One proposal, along these lines, is (in effect) from C. I. Lewis; we can get a stronger conditional than the material conditional by using our alethic-necessity operator *necessarily*. In particular, assuming the treatment of the Box from Chapter 11, we can define (just for convenient abbreviation) $A \Rightarrow B$ to be $\Box(A \to B)$, where $\to$ is our material conditional (and, so, $A \to B$ is defined as $\neg A \lor B$). Our truth/falsity conditions for $A \Rightarrow B$ are as you'd expect:

- $[c, w] \models_1 A \Rightarrow B$ iff $[c, w'] \models_1 A \to B$ for all w' in c.
- $[c, w] \models_0 A \Rightarrow B$ iff $[c, w'] \models_0 A \to B$ for some w' in c.

Hence, $A \Rightarrow B$ is true at a world (in a case) if and only if at *every* world (in the given case) either A is false there or B is true there.[1] This delivers what we wanted: the mere falsity of the antecedent or truth of the consequent is insufficient for the truth of the (stronger) conditional; an all-worlds connection between the two is required. (Question: on this stronger account of 'if', what do you say about previous Barack-Obama conditional? Is it true? false? neither? what?)

What this shows is that, at least if we already have a suitable alethic-necessity connective, we can define a conditional that is stronger than the material conditional.[2]

One question to consider (though, for space reasons, not considered here), is whether our stronger, all-worlds-material conditional gets everything right. After all, consider a sentence with a necessarily false antecedent: *if 1=0 then all suffering will be eliminated by the year 2012*. If we read the given 'if' as $\Rightarrow$, then the given conditional is true at all worlds, since the corresponding material conditional—in effect, *either* $1 \neq 0$ *or all suffering will be eliminated by the year 2012*—is true at all worlds. (Why?) Maybe this sort of result is right for some conditionals, but, at least intuitively, it seems that there is a common sense of 'if' on which *if 1=0 then all suffering will be eliminated by the year 2012* is simply false. A task for the philosophical logician, then, is to come up with a better account of the conditional, or at least come up with yet another conditional that can be false even when its antecedent is 'false everywhere' (so to speak).

There are many different routes one might go towards solving this sort of problem. Further reading is provided to set you along further paths. For now, even though we've barely touched the huge and philosophically significant topic of conditionals, we briefly turn to another topic: negation.

« *Parenthetical remark.* The array of conditional-related phenomena, relevant to logical theory, is vast. For a tiny glimpse into the vastness see Bennett 2003, Gauker 2005, Lycan 2001, Mares 2004,

---

[1] The minimal-hyphenation policy from Chapter 11 remains in effect concerning some of our *truth at* relations.

[2] This needn't mean that *exactly one* of the two conditionals is 'the real conditional', whatever that might mean. Instead, we may simply have various conditionals in the language. (I will not elaborate on this point, but it also applies to other connectives briefly discussed below.)

Priest 2008, Read 1989, Sider 2009, and also sources cited in the given bibliographies. *End parenthetical.* »

12.2   Other negations

Another fruitful area for logical theorizing concerns negations. As in previous chapters, the classical story of negation has it that, for every sentence A, either A or its negation $\neg A$ is true, and that we never have A and $\neg A$ true. The 'basic gappy' account (see Chapter 5) agrees that we never have both A and $\neg A$ true for any sentence A, but it rejects the exhaustiveness thesis that either A or $\neg A$ is true for all A. In turn, the 'basic glutty' theory (one that, say, doesn't posit gaps) agrees with the classical theory that negation is exhaustive, but it rejects the exclusivity thesis that we never have A and $\neg A$ true for any A.

Logical theorizing about negation can—and often does—go further. We might think that we have more than one negation-like connective in our language. Suppose, for example, that we embrace the basic gappy and glutty account of negation, the account reflected in the FDE theory (see Chapter 6). (We can ignore worlds for present purposes.) On this theory, we have neither exhaustion (viz., LEM) nor explosion (viz., EFQ):

$$\nvdash A \vee \neg A$$

and

$$A, \neg A \nvdash B$$

At this stage, a question, largely concerned with 'gaps', arises: what negation-like connective are we using when we truly say that some A is gappy—that A is *not* true and *not* false? In the FDE theory, falsity is simply truth of our regular negation connective: A is false just if $\neg A$ is true. Hence, if we are using $\neg$ when we say that A is *not* true and *not* false, we are asserting something of the form

$$\neg A \wedge \neg \neg A$$

Now, in the FDE theory, we don't have explosion, and so this sort of (inconsistent) claim doesn't lead to absurdity by implying that every sentence B is true. Still, there's a problem. To see the problem, recall the truth conditions for $\neg$ in our FDE theory (see

Chapter 6), and in particular what happens when A is 'gappy'. On those truth conditions, if A is gappy (modeled by a case c such that $c \not\models_1 A$ and $c \not\models_0 A$), then so too are both $\neg A$ and $\neg\neg A$. (Again, look back to the truth conditions for $\neg$ in Chapter 6.) Moreover, according to the FDE theory, the truth conditions for $\wedge$ are such that a conjunction $\neg A \wedge \neg\neg A$ is gappy if both $\neg A$ and $\neg\neg A$ are gappy. (See Chapter 6 truth conditions for $\wedge$.) What all of this tells us is that, according to the FDE theory, $\neg A \wedge \neg\neg A$ is gappy if A itself is gappy.

So what? Well, we were after a sense of 'not' (or, as above, a negation-like connective) that allows us to *truly* say that A is gappy—to truly say that A is *not* true and *not* false, where the falsity of A amounts to the truth of $\neg A$. The foregoing discussion of FDE truth conditions for $\neg$ plainly show that $\neg$ itself will not do the job.[3]

What, then, shall we do to find our new 'not'? One course might be to change the truth conditions of $\neg$ employed in the FDE theory. One might think, though, that the FDE theory of negation is correct; the trouble, one might think, is that we need to acknowledge a different negation-like connective in addition to our regular FDE negation. Towards this end, we might introduce a (unary) connective η into the syntax. The question is: what truth (and falsity) conditions should it get in the basic gappy and glutty setting? There are different answers available, and correspondingly different logical theories. One constraint, of course, is that ηA be true if A is gappy. (See the issue above for why we're imposing this constraint!) Along these lines, here is one natural thought. (Coming up with alternative truth conditions that satisfy the given constraint is left as an exercise.)

- $c \models_1 \eta A$ iff $c \not\models_1 A$.
- $c \models_0 \eta A$ iff $c \models_1 A$.

Assuming that everything else (connectives, consequence, etc.) is treated as per FDE, this gives us some notable logical behavior for our negation-like connective.

---

[3]I should note that I'm simplifying matters. One could put the weight of the problem on a new notion of 'true' rather than on a sense of 'not' (not that these need be wildly different in the end). These matters are too advanced for discussion here, but see Field 2008 for a thorough discussion.

- Exhaustion (for η): $\vdash A \vee \eta A$

- Explosion (for η): $A, \eta A \vdash B$

That we have Exhaustion for η may be seen as follows. The only way for $A \vee \eta A$ to be untrue is for both disjuncts to be untrue. But, given the truth conditions for η above, there can't be a case in which both A and ηA are untrue. After all, if we have $c \not\models_1 A$ then $c \models_1 \eta A$. So, every case is one in which either A or ηA is true. For Explosion (for η), note that, as the truth condition for η shows, we can never have a case c in which $c \models_1 A$ and $c \models_1 \eta A$, and so we can never have a counterexample to arguments from A and ηA to B. (The truth condition for η tells us that, for any case c, if we have $c \models_1 \eta A$ then $c \not\models_1 A$. So, we can't have both ηA and A being true-in-a-case.)

This new negation-like connective does the desired task: we can truly say that A is gappy—neither true nor false (i.e., not true and its normal negation not true)—by using η so understood; we can assert $\eta A \wedge \eta \neg A$, which, as can be verified by looking at the above truth/falsity conditions, is true-in-c if c is a case in which A is neither true nor false.

Of course, as with life in general, so too in philosophical logic: resolving one issue often leaves other issues to resolve. One among many issue(s) is whether Explosion for η should ultimately be avoided. If, for example, one considers Liar-like sentences involving η (e.g., a sentence saying of itself that it's *not* true, where 'not' is along η lines), then one might think that we have to allow for η-involving gluts, in which case Explosion for η should fail. (See Chapter 6 for discussion involving $\neg$, and apply it to η.) Ultimately, this is a matter for theoretical debate, and in particular debate on the role of η in the language and about the overall features of the given language in general. This is too much to go into here; however, it is notable that a simple tweak to the above truth conditions for η gets rid of Explosion. In particular, suppose that we give the following truth condition (leaving the falsity condition as above):

- $c \models_1 \eta A$ iff $c \models_0 A$ or $c \not\models_1 A$ (or both).

This tweak delivers a countermodel to Explosion for η. How? The answer is left to you (viz., the reader). For now, we briefly turn to one more example of a logical connective that one might theorize about: actuality.

« *Parenthetical remark.* I should note, before moving on, that one of the most famous non-classical theories of negation is that of *intuitionistic logic*, which is motivated directly out of a particular philosophy of mathematics (notably, intuitionism). This is well worth your exploration. Alas, giving a short, 'basic', but adequate treatment here would require more space than is available, and so the matter is left for further reading. *End parenthetical.* »

12.3   Other alethic modalities: actuality

In Chapter 11 we briefly looked at a few alethic modalities: necessity (in a very broad sense) and, derivatively, possibility. These notions were treated as unary connectives that quantified over 'possible worlds'. In turn, we defined *truth in a case* in terms of a special *actual world* of the given case. Intuitively, there's one 'real' universe of worlds (and our formal, world-filled cases serve, in some way, as different models of the one 'real' universe); and within this real universe of worlds, we inhabit exactly one such world—the so-called actual world. In some worlds (of the real universe), you are 14-feet tall, even though *actually* you're less than 14-feet tall.

The issue is how to model this *actuality* connective, *it is actually true that...* or *in the actual world...* or, simply, *actually....* For present purposes, we look only at a very simple—though entirely natural—proposal.[4]

Suppose that we add a unary connective ∇ to the language. We want to interpret it as our actuality operator. Let us leave our formal picture as per the Mfde framework (see Chapter 11), so that our cases contain not only a set of worlds W but also the so-called actual world @. In this sort of set up, a natural idea gives ∇A the following truth conditions.

- $[c, w] \models_1 \nabla A$ iff $[c, @] \models_1 A$.
- $[c, w] \models_0 \nabla A$ iff $[c, @] \models_0 A$.

---

[4]Note well: the philosophy of actuality is a controversial topic—and I here skip the controversy by simply sketching one simple idea on the matter. See Lewis 1970; Lewis 1986.

On this account, ∇A is true at a world just if—as you'd expect—
A is true at the actual world, and similarly false at a world just if
A is false at the actual world. This has the happy result that ∇A
implies A and vice versa. (Explain, by invoking the relevant definition of validity, why this result holds!) On the other hand, we
happily get that $\Diamond A$ does not imply ∇A: just because A is true
at *some* world, it hardly follows that A is true at the (unique) actual world. (Question: does $\Box A$ imply ∇A on the current account,
where $\Box A$ is treated along Mfde lines?)

As with most topics, there is room for debate about whether
actuality should be treated as above, or even whether there is
more than one notion of actuality in the language. All of this is
left to your future logical investigations.

We now briefly turn to another road towards different logical
theories, this one being somewhat more revisionary, with respect
to earlier chapters, than the foregoing.

12.4   Same connectives, different truth conditions

So far, we have touched on the idea of expanding the language
with different connectives while leaving the rest of the connectives as in previous chapters. One might instead give an entirely
different account of truth/faslity conditions, even for the basic
connectives (conjunction, negation, disjunction). For simplicity,
we illustrate the idea only with respect to the given basic connectives.

For present purposes, we look at only one motivation for
changing our basic FDE picture, and briefly look at the resulting
picture.

The main question concerns our philosophical ideas about
'gaps'. In Chapter 5 (and forward), we thought of gaps as meaningful sentences that, for one reason or another, were neither true
nor false. What if, instead, we think of gaps as syntactically well-
formed but nonetheless *meaningless* (declarative) sentences? In
other words, we can think of gappy sentences as grammatical,
declarative sentences that, for one reason or another, are meaningless.

We can still keep our broad FDE categories of true, false,
glutty, and gappy; it's just that now our *gappy* category com-

prises *meaningless* sentences. This different philosophical picture of our 'gaps' motivates different truth conditions for our basic connectives from that in the FDE theory (see Chapter 6). In particular, if we have an entirely *meaningless* (though syntactically kosher) sentence A, then this very meaninglessness will infect any molecular sentence made from the given meaningless sentence. If A is meaningless, then how can $A \lor B$ or $A \land B$ or even $\neg A$ be meaningful? In short: if you've got a meaningless sentence, the conjunction (similarly disjunction, negation) of it with anything else is going to be meaningless—or so one way of thinking goes.

Whether all of this is ultimately correct is for further debate to tell. What is notable here is that the different philosophical conception motivates different truth conditions for our various basic connectives. For present purposes, we can let the truth conditions for negation remain as in the FDE theory. (Why are the FDE truth/falsity conditions compatible with the current conception of 'gaps' qua meaningless? Hint: in FDE, A is gappy iff $\neg A$ is gappy. So, if we're now simply thinking of our 'gaps' as meaningless, the clause for negation can remain as it was, except informally reinterpreted: A is meaningless iff $\neg A$ is meaningless.) What, though, of disjunctions and conjunctions? In FDE, a disjunction is true so long as at least one disjunct is true, *even if* the other disjunct is gappy. This clashes with the conception of gaps above, according to which all molecular sentences are ultimately meaningless if one of their subsentences is meaningless. Similarly, a conjunction, on FDE, is false if at least one conjunct is false, *even if* the other conjunct is gappy. So, this too clashes with the thought that a molecular sentence cannot be true or false if one of its subsentences is meaningless.

Given all of this, one approach to the truth/falsity conditions for disjunctions and conjunctions is as follows. (Here, we ignore worlds. As an additional exercise, you can fill out the fuller picture with predicates, quantifiers, etc., and worlds!) For convenience, let us use $c \models_! A$ as shorthand for *either $c \models_1 A$ or $c \models_0 A$*.

- Conjunction.

  $c \models_1 A \land B$ iff $c \models_1 A$ and $c \models_1 B$.

  $c \models_0 A \land B$ iff $c \models_! A$, $c \models_! B$, and either $c \models_0 A$ or $c \models_0 B$.

- Disjunction.

  $c \models_1 A \vee B$ iff $c \models_! A$, $c \models_! B$, and either $c \models_1 A$ or $c \models_1 B$.

  $c \models_0 A \vee B$ iff $c \models_0 A$ and $c \models_0 B$.

These are slightly long-winded, but they do the trick. Notice, for example, that there's no case in which a disjunction is true (or false) if either disjunct is gappy (i.e., 'meaningless'). The same goes for conjunctions. (Verify both claims!)

Does this give us the same logical theory as FDE? There are similarities (e.g., no LEM or EFQ), but there are also notable differences. One striking difference is that so-called Addition no longer holds: the form $A \therefore A \vee B$ is no longer valid. A counterexample is a case in which A is true but B meaningless! Other differences are left for the reader's discovery.

12.5   Another road to difference: consequence

As works in 'further reading' attest, there are many roads towards different logical theories. In this chapter, we've looked at two ways of diverging from the logical theories discussed in previous chapters: one is to expand by adding new logical expressions; the other is to keep the same lot of logical expressions but revise the semantics (e.g., the truth/falsity conditions for the connectives). And you can think of variations on these themes.

One other notable route should be mentioned (though, for space reasons, not discussed): one could keep both the lot of logical expressions and their semantics the same as in previous chapters, but *change the definition of logical consequence!* For example, consider the basic gappy theory K_3 (we have gaps but no gluts), but suppose that we add an additional constraint on validity (or logical consequence): instead of requiring only that there be no case in which all premises are true and conclusion untrue, we also require that there be no case in which the conclusion is false but not all premises false. (This is sometimes called the requirement of 'falsity-preservation backwards'.) This minor change in the definition of *consequence* has an impact. By way of illustration, consider the following argument form.

$$A \wedge \neg A \therefore (A \wedge \neg A) \wedge B$$

This is valid in K_3. After all, on the basic paracomplete (i.e., K_3) theory, there can't be a counterexample to the given argument form, since there's no K_3 case in which $A \wedge \neg A$ is true, and hence the form is valid. *On the other hand*, if we now also require—according to the falsity-preservation-backwards suggestion above—that any K_3 case in which $(A \wedge \neg A) \wedge B$ is false is one in which $A \wedge \neg A$ is false, then the argument is no longer valid (on the revised account of validity). After all, just consider a K_3 case c such that $c \models_0 B$ but $c \not\models_1 A$ and $c \not\models_0 A$. (In other words, we're considering a K_3 case in which B is false but A is a gap.) According to the K_3 falsity conditions for conjunctions, $(A \wedge \neg A) \wedge B$ is false-in-c, that is, $c \models_0 (A \wedge \neg A) \wedge B$. But, since A is a gap in c, we have that $A \wedge \neg A$ is a gap in c, that is, that $c \not\models_0 A \wedge \neg A$. So, on the revised—stricter (falsity-preservation-backwards)—account of consequence, the given argument form is no longer valid.

A simpler example of the effect of modifying our definition of consequence in various ways is as follows. Concentrate on the basic classical theory bc (see Chapter 4). In this theory, Explosion (EFQ) is valid:

$$A \wedge \neg A \vdash_{bc} B$$

Suppose, however, that we modify the bc account of consequence by requiring not only that there be no bc case in which the premises are true and conclusion untrue, but—for purposes of ruling out vacuity or the 'null situation' (as some might say)—we also require that there be at least one bc case in which the premises are all true. This has an immediate effect on the resulting consequence relation. To see this, note that the Explosion form $A \wedge \neg A \therefore B$ is now invalid (on the resulting theory). That this is so is left as an exercise. (Hint: if validity, on the new definition, now also requires a bc case in which all premises are true, the issue of Explosion turns on whether there is a bc case in which $A \wedge \neg A$ is true.)

Summary and looking behind and ahead

Summary. This chapter has highlighted a few different routes towards logical theories that differ from the ones sketched in this book. The highlights in this chapter barely scratch the surface of different directions that logical theories might take, let alone the many interesting phenomena that might serve to motivate different logical theories. Still, this chapter serves to point in basic directions: changing the stock of logical expressions; changing the truth conditions of various connectives (or expressions, in general); and changing the definition of consequence. All of these directions can open up new and interesting logical theories, and you're encouraged to so open up!

Looking Behind—and Forward. Since this is the last chapter in the book, we now look behind but also briefly forward (to further studies beyond this book). We have, throughout, explored various logical theories concerning basic logical expressions. While the theories themselves may disagree with one another along various lines, all of them are united in the basic recipe for logical consequence: absence of counterexample—absence of a 'case' in which the premises are true and conclusion untrue. Getting clear on the logical resources of the language (the stock of logical expressions) and, in turn, the appropriate truth-in-a-case conditions for the expressions is a large task in specifying logical consequence. What this book has illustrated, I hope, is that the task is not only informed by philosophical considerations; it thrives on them.

This book will have accomplished its goal (or, at least, a goal) if you're not only still reading it but you're inspired to do more work in logical theory. There are many open and unexplored logical roads to pursue. In the spirit of exploration, I encourage you to go forth! Still, as a next step—and, I must admit, I feel a bit like Dumbledore sending Harry back to the Dursleys' house for the summer—you should probably turn to a proper first course in classical first-order logic. These courses are available at any proper university, and widely available via numerous textbooks. After getting a proper first-order logic course in you (and, if you choose to really go forth in logic, a proper classical first-order metatheory course), you should consider pursuing any of the 'further reading' works, and moving onward and upward from there!

Further Reading. There are many, many, many areas of logical exploration that have not been mentioned in this book. Not only are there many different ways of doing 'semantics' (or model theory) that have not been considered here; there is a very important—some would say *the most important*—area of logic that has not been touched (viz., proof theory or deductive systems). But such matters are now open to you. To get a sense of what's out there, it may be most useful to work through a few surveys: Goble 2001 is an excellent source from which you can get a basic sense of many logical areas—intuitionistic logic, quantum logic, relevant logic, second- (and higher-) order logic, and much, much more. Other handbooks of philosophical logic are also available (Jacquette, 2002), along with a much wider and more advanced multi-volume collection (Gabbay and Günthner, 2001). Also, in addition to the few textbooks mentioned in 'further reading' in previous chapters (Beall and van Fraassen, 2003; Priest, 2008; Restall, 2005), other recent textbooks have emerged that may be useful (Bell, DeVidi and Solomon, 2001; Burgess, 2009; Sider, 2009). An ever-so-small effort will reveal many logic textbooks from which you can learn a great deal more—and, indeed, a great deal more about the 'basics' of logical theory. Look about and enjoy! The universe of logical options is in front of you. . .

Exercises

1. Prove that $\nabla A \vdash A$ and $A \vdash \nabla A$ (i.e., that our Actuality operator, defined above, both Captures and Releases).

2. Do we have that $\Box A \vdash \nabla A$ in the Mfde theory (expanded with ∇ as above)? If so, prove it. If not, give a counterexample.

3. Using the revised truth conditions (see page 166), give a countermodel to η-Explosion: viz., $A, \eta A \therefore B$.

4. With respect to the 'meaningless' approach to disjunction (see §12.4), provide a case in which A is true but $A \vee B$ not true (for some A and B).

5. How does the 'meaningless' approach (see §12.4) compare with Weak Kleene (see Chapter 5 exercises)?

6. Fill out the 'meaningless' approach (see §12.4) by adding predicates, quantifiers, and a necessity operator. (NB: there may be more than one way of doing this that is consistent with the basic 'meaningless' idea.)

7. Invoking the definitions of 'contingent' and 'broadly contingent' from Chapter 5 exercises, give what you think are the right truth- and falsity-in-a-case conditions for a *contingency* operator in the otherwise Mfde setting. (In other words: add new unary connectives to serve as an *it is contingent that...* and *it is broadly contingent that...* operators in the otherwise Mfde setting. What is the logic of your connective(s) like? Explore!

8. How might you add a *necessarily consistent* connective to the Mfde? What should the truth conditions for *it is necessarily consistent...* be in a broad Mfde setting? What about defining our target 'necessarily consistent' operator in Mfde thus: just let $\mathbb{C}A$ abbreviate $\Box\neg(A \wedge \neg A)$. What, then, is the logic of $\mathbb{C}$ in Mfde? Are there Mfde cases in which $\mathbb{C}A$ is a *glut*—and, so, true but itself 'inconsistent' (since also false)? Is this a problem for a consistency operator?

9. What other phenomena might motivate different logics? Think and explore!

Sample answers

Answer 2. Yes, $\Box A$ implies ∇A in the Mfde theory (expanded with the given actuality operator). To see this, consider any case c such that $[c, @] \models_1 \Box A$, in which case—by the Mfde truth conditions for the box—every world w in the given universe (case) is one at which A is true, that is, $[c, w] \not\models_1 A$ (for all w in the universe). Hence, in particular, A is true at $@$, that is, $[c, @] \models_1 A$. But, then, given the truth conditions for ∇, we have that $[c, @] \models_1 \nabla A$. What we've shown here is that any (Mfde) case in which $\Box A$ is true is one in which ∇A is true (given the going truth conditions for ∇). What we've shown, in other words, is that $\Box A$ implies ∇A.

APPENDIX A

List of Common Abbreviations

This appendix lists a few of the abbreviations commonly used in this book, and indicates the page on which they first appear.

$\vdash_{bc}$. (General) Basic Classical Consequence, page 54.

$\vdash_x$. Consequence relation for theory X, page 54.

$\vdash_{K3}$. (General, Basic, and Beyond) Paracomplete (Strong Kleene, K3) Consequence, page 70.

$\vdash_{FDE}$. (General, Basic, and Beyond) Paraconsistent (FDE) Consequence, page 86, and page 90.

$\vdash_{bc}^=$. (General) Basic Classical Consequence with Identity, page 116.

$\vdash_{K3}^=$. (General) Basic Paracomplete Consequence with Identity, page 116.

$\vdash_{FDE}^=$. (General) Basic Paraconsistent (FDE) Consequence with Identity, page 116.

Mfde. (Free) Modal paracomplete and paraconsistent theory (with identity, quantifiers), page 150.

REFERENCES

Anderson, Alan Ross and Belnap, Nuel D. (1975). *Entailment: The Logic of Relevance and Necessity*, Volume 1. Princeton University Press, Princeton.

Anderson, Alan Ross, Belnap, Nuel D., and Dunn, J. Michael (1992). *Entailment: The Logic of Relevance and Necessity*, Volume 2. Princeton University Press, Princeton.

Asenjo, F. G. (1966). A calculus of antinomies. *Notre Dame Journal of Formal Logic*, **16**, 103–105.

Barwise, Jon (1989). Situations, facts, and true propositions. In *The Situation in Logic*, Number 17 in CSLI Lecture Notes, pp. 221–254. CSLI Publications, Stanford, CA.

Barwise, Jon and Perry, John (1983). *Situations and Attitudes*. MIT Press, Bradford Books, Cambridge, MA.

Beall, Jc (2009). *Spandrels of Truth*. Oxford University Press, Oxford.

Beall, Jc and Restall, Greg (2005). *Logical Pluralism*. Oxford University Press, Oxford.

Beall, Jc and van Fraassen, Bas C. (2003). *Possibilities and Paradox: An Introduction to Modal and Many-Valued Logic*. Oxford University Press, Oxford.

Bell, John L., DeVidi, David, and Solomon, Graham (2001). *Logical Options: An Introduction to Classical and Alternative Logics*. Broadview Press.

Bennett, Jonathan (2003). *A Philosophical Guide to Conditionals*. Oxford University Press, Oxford.

Burgess, John P. (2009). *Philosophical Logic*. Princeton University Press, Princeton, NJ.

Chellas, Brian F. (1980). *Modal Logic: An Introduction*. Cambridge University Press, Cambridge.

Church, Alonzo (1956). *Introduction to Mathematical Logic*. Princeton Mathematical Series. Princeton University Press, Princeton. Originally published in 1944 in the Annals of Mathematical Studies. The latest reprinting, in the Princeton Landmarks in Mathematics Series, is 1996.

Copeland, B. J. (2002). The genesis of possible world semantics. *Journal of Philosophical Logic*, **31**, 99–137.

Field, Hartry (2008). *Saving Truth from Paradox*. Oxford University Press, Oxford.

Gabbay, Dov M. and Günthner, Franz (ed.) (2001). *Handbook of Philosophical Logic* (Second edn). Springer, Netherlands. NB: 2001 marks the publication of the first few volumes in this multi-volume collection; other volumes appear in later years.

Gauker, Christopher (2005). *Conditionals in Context*. Bradford Books. MIT, Cambridge, MA.

Girle, Rod (2000). *Modal Logics and Philosophy*. McGill-Queen's University Press, London.

Goble, Lou (ed.) (2001). *The Blackwell Guide to Philosophical Logic*. Blackwell, Oxford.

Goldrei, D. C. (1996). *Classic Set Theory: A Guided Independent Study*. Chapman & Hall/CRC.

Haack, Susan (1978). *Philosophy of Logics*. Cambridge University Press.

——— (1996). *Deviant Logic, Fuzzy Logic: Beyond the Formalism*. Cambridge University Press, Cambridge.

Hughes, G. and Cresswell, M. (1996). *A New Introduction to Modal Logic*. Routledge, London.

Hyde, Dominic (2008). *Vagueness, Logic, and Ontology*. Ashgate, Aldershot.

Jacquette, Dale (ed.) (2002). *A Companion to Philosophical Logic*. Blackwell Publishers, Oxford.

Keefe, Rosanna and Smith, Peter (ed.) (1997). *Vagueness: A Reader*. MIT Press, Cambridge, MA.

Kripke, Saul A. (1972). *Naming and Necessity*. Harvard University Press, Cambridge, MA.

Lambert, Karel (2003). *Free Logic: Selected Essays*. Cambridge University Press, Cambridge.

Lewis, David (1970). Anselm and actuality. *Nous*, 175–188. Reprinted in (Lewis, 1983).

———— (1983). *Philosophical Papers*, Volume I. Oxford University Press, Oxford.

———— (1986). *On the Plurality of Worlds*. Blackwell, Oxford.

Lycan, William G. (2001). *Real Conditionals*. Oxford University Press, Oxford.

Mares, Edwin (2004). *Relevant Logic: A Philosophical Interpretation*. Cambridge University Press, Cambridge.

Menzel, Christopher (1991). The true modal logic. *Journal of Philosophical Logic*, **20**, 331–374.

Priest, Graham (1979). The logic of paradox. *Journal of Philosophical Logic*, **8**, 219–241.

———— (2006). *In Contradiction* (Second edn). Oxford University Press, Oxford.

———— (2008). *An Introduction to Non-Classical Logic* (Second edn). Cambridge University Press, Cambridge.

Read, Stephen (1989). *Relevant Logic: A Philosophical Examination of Inference*. Blackwell, Oxford.

———— (1995). *Thinking about Logic*. Oxford University Press.

Restall, Greg (2005). *Logic: An Introduction*. New York: Routledge.

Russell, Bertrand (1901). Recent works on the principles of mathematics. *The International Monthly*, **5**, 83–101. Reprinted in Russell 1918.

———— (1918). *Mysticism and Logic, and other essays*. Longmans, Green and Co., New York.

Sainsbury, R. M. (2001). *Logical Forms* (Second edn). Wiley-Blackwell, Oxford.

Sider, Theodore (2009). *Logic for Philosophy*. Oxford University Press.

Smith, Nicholas J. J. (2008). *Vagueness and Degrees of Truth*. Oxford University Press, Oxford.

Smith, Peter (2003). *An Introduction to Formal Logic*. Cambridge University Press, Cambridge.

Williamson, Timothy (1994). *Vagueness*. Routledge, Oxford.

INDEX